WHAT IT MEANS TO BE A DESIGNER TODAY

What It Means to Be a Designer Today

PRINCETON ARCHITECTURAL PRESS · NEW YORK

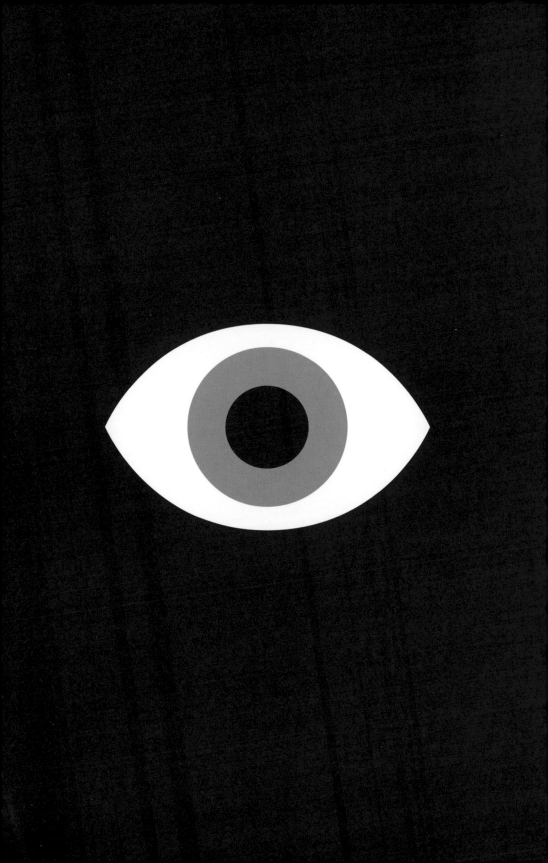

Reflections, Questions, and Ideas from AIGA's Eye on Design

EDITED BY

Liz Stinson and Jarrett Fuller

CONTENTS

CONTENTS

INTRODUCTION

In 2014, when AIGA first began publishing *Eye on Design*, the publication was meant to fill a gap in the design writing landscape. There were few venues thoughtfully covering the work of talented young designers, and even fewer that explored the issues they cared about with the journalistic rigor expected in other subject areas. From the start, *Eye on Design* was meant to be a publication that could celebrate and interrogate the design world and its dynamics.

In those early days, the world was in a different place. Design was in the middle of a cultural renaissance, and people were excited by the simple idea of celebrating creativity. As the world changed, so did *Eye on Design* and the way we thought about design's connection to the broader cultural and political shifts happening around us. It required that *Eye on Design* move beyond "design inspiration," and that's exactly what we did.

Eye on Design evolved into an expansive editorial platform that reaches across digital, publication, and event sectors. But even as the way we tell stories has changed, our North Star has remained fixed. This book is our attempt to bridge *Eye on Design*'s past with its present. This collection of essays, conversations, and reported stories—both old and new—is meant to tell a bigger story of what it means to be a designer today, in all its complexity.

The book is organized around three broad themes that define the work we've produced over the years. We begin with "Reflections": the events, trends, and movements that serve as critical points in recent design history, all filtered through the reporting of our correspondents. The "Questions" section follows, and is where we ask (and answer) questions that challenge assumptions and push for a more equitable, generous, and thoughtful design landscape. Lastly, we explore "Ideas," the big ideas that interrogate design's present and ultimately dictate its future.

You'll notice at the top of certain pieces throughout the book a time stamp signifying when the story was first published on *Eye on Design*'s website or in *Eye on Design* magazine; alongside some of those pieces is an introduction by the author to situate the story in the current moment. We believe these previously published stories stand the test of time and add to the continuing narrative of the new pieces. Because while journalism is a snapshot, it's also an ongoing story that, when pieced together, can help us better understand where we've been and where we're going.

In the process of compiling these essays, reports, and conversations, connective tissue began to emerge. Throughout the book, you'll notice thematic echoes—and polite disagreements—that are accompanied by little nudges that lead you, the reader, to weave in and out of the sections as you follow the thread of what's most interesting to you. This way of navigating a book felt true to what we've always tried to do at *Eye on Design*. Our goal has never been to tell readers how they should think about something. Rather, we hope that the stories here will serve as a prism through which designers and non-designers alike can start to make sense of their world.

FOREWORD
PERRIN DRUMM

I was recently out of the country on a short but long-overdue vacation—no family obligations, no work emails, just a rare week of pure non-itinerized enjoyment. I was traveling with Tala Safié, *Eye on Design*'s first intern, who designed the inaugural issue of the print magazine and shaped the visual language of the site's approach to journalism (she has since become an art director at the *New York Times* and helped us with the creative direction of this book). I was talking with a local I had just met, a designer (of course) who was listing off the sites he read, and the first one he mentioned was *Eye on Design*. He liked how it published stories that went beyond the typical "design inspo" fluff, and asked if I knew it. Yeah, I knew it. I started it.

In 2014, with scant funding and a lot of favors begged of design friends, I convinced AIGA, the hundred-plus-year-old organization where I had just been hired, to let me try something new. I wanted to tell the kinds of design stories I wasn't seeing anywhere else, but that I knew people cared about and wanted to read. Most of my friends were designers, so I had a behind-the-scenes look at what actually went on behind the glossy Photoshop curtain—a perspective I didn't see reflected in the current crop of publications. Like many readers, I was tired of design hero worship (gross), the senseless infighting over logo redesigns (boring), and all of the genuflecting at the altar of Swiss Modernism. There was so much more out there—why wasn't anyone writing about it?

I was meeting designers who (shock!) didn't go to design school, and whose world wasn't shaped by myopic Twitter wars over typeface applications. These were people with nuanced points of view who were as passionate about bigger, broader issues as they were about pixels and picas. Let's hear from them, I thought. In other words, let's tell stories about what it really means to be a designer today. It seems obvious now, but at the time, publishing those perspectives was just not a done thing.

Since then, *Eye on Design* has become a place where some of the most talented and thoughtful writers, editors, designers, and generally visually creative people I could have only dreamed of working with have gathered to share stories, celebrate exciting work, and lend a critical point of view. Together, collectively, they have transformed the humble pink-eyed platform I dreamed up into a rich forum for discussion, debate, and incisive conversation.

Back when I was working on it alone, spending nights and weekends trying to get it off the ground (under the raised eyebrows of colleagues who warned me that no one would take such a friendly-looking site seriously), I never thought that a decade later I'd be sitting in a café four thousand miles from home with a designer who was not only excited to share their thoughts on the latest article, but proud to name-check *Eye on Design*, like a badge of honor.

With Tala sitting just a few chairs away, it was a full-circle, deeply humbling moment. I may have plugged the site in, so to speak, but without the community that grew up around it, *Eye on Design* would never have become the special blend of smart reporting, personal storytelling, unexpected perspectives, and forward-looking journalism that is only possible when many voices join together. It's a rare thing in media culture to be able to carve out a space like this.

Someone once told me that if you want to go fast, go alone. But if you want to go far, go with others. In these pages, you'll hear from people who are forging new paths, who are exploring new ideas and expanding the design landscape for us all, who understand that design is most impactful when you move off your desktop and out into the world. I hope you'll join in and come along.

PART I : REFLECTIONS

INTRODUCTION

ho? What? When? Where? Why?

Any journalist will tell you that all good stories begin by answering the "five W's." These questions might seem straight-forward, but they are a means to gather essential information and provide a framework for understanding a story's deeper meaning and context.

Context is everything when writing about design. It can help explain aesthetic phenomena like our obsession with minimal-ism; it can shed light on the dynamics driving the burgeoning freelancer economy. Though design stories are often told through the lens of a designed object, the best stories are often about the why and the how—not so much the what—of it all.

Design journalism, like any journalism, is an attempt to crystallize a moment in time. The stories in this section are all rooted in a particular time and place. They are snapshots of an event, a project, a person, or an idea that feels inextricably bound to the moment during which it existed in the world.

If You Love It, Let It Go (All Media Is Design Media)

by Jarrett Fuller

"t happened again," the voice-over says. The camera holds on a man in a blue-lit room, waking from a nightmare in a cold sweat. Then it cuts to his kitchen: he's staring into space, and his partner standing behind is clearly worried about him. Now he's driving to work, unable to focus. "I forgot about it for years," the voice-over continues. "Then I remembered that *Avatar*, the giant international blockbuster, used the Papyrus font as its logo."

This is not a scene from the life of an obsessive graphic designer or a story retold on an otherwise sleepy graphic design subreddit. The man is Ryan Gosling, and we're watching a skit from the forty-third season premiere of *Saturday Night Live* in 2017. "He clicked the drop-down menu," Gosling says, "and he just randomly selected—Papyrus." From there, Gosling spirals, unable to control his emotions regarding the widely ridiculed typeface. The video quickly circulated among designers, but its resonance reached far wider. Designers and non-designers alike got the joke. Here was *Saturday Night Live*—prime-time network television!—talking about a font. Graphic design, it seemed, had reached popular culture.

Ryan Gosling waxing poetic about Papyrus didn't come out of nowhere. Almost as soon as Apple put a font menu in the first desktop Macintosh, graphic design was on a path away from the esoteric skills of the select few and becoming a tool for the masses. Within a few years, nearly everyone had opinions on fonts, and the skills to whip up a custom invite for their child's birthday party.

When the *New York Times* changed the article font for the newspaper in 2003, its front page read:

1 **W. A. Dwiggins, "New Kind of Printing Calls for New Design" (1923), in** *Layout in Advertising*, **ed. Lester Beall (New York: Museum of Modern Art, 1937), 9–17.**

"Notice anything? More than the news is new today on the front page and in the main news sections" (a full story on page C8 explained the changes, with a full history of their new typeface, Cheltenham). After Tropicana redesigned the packaging of its orange juice in 2009, there was significant enough outrage that they backtracked and reverted to the old design. A few months later, Gap did the same thing. In 2010, rapper-turned-provocateur Kanye West tweeted, "Sometimes I get emotional over fonts." The popular meme "Graphic design is my passion" was used on Twitter by a major Senate candidate in 2022 in response to his opponent.

Design, in many ways, has become the buzzword of our time—alongside words like "innovation" and "disruption"—and with that pervasiveness, an entire media ecosystem developed around it. This wasn't always the case. It's thought that a California School of Arts and Crafts (now CalArts) professor first coined the term "graphic design" in 1917 and that typesetter and printer William Addison Dwiggins later popularized it—within the industry, that is—in his 1923 essay "New Kind of Printing Calls for New Design."[1] Then for most of the next century, the majority of the discourse around graphic design continued to be relegated to the field itself: designers talking to other designers. This followed in the tradition of the trade journals focused on printing, typesetting, illustration, and advertising that were being published as early as the 1850s. AIGA, founded in 1914 as the American Institute of Graphic Arts, published its first annual, with Frederic Goudy as editor, in 1922. *Print* magazine, which still exists today, albeit as a decidedly non-print website, began in 1940 as a quarterly journal for designers to demonstrate "the far reaching importance of the graphic arts."

Then finally, as graphic design education programs matured, so, too, did a more academic discourse separate from the trade magazines. *Design Issues*, launched in 1984, was the first US-based academic journal to examine the history, theory, and criticism of design. At this time, many graphic designers saw the changing landscape of the field: Photoshop 1.0—released in 1990 for $850 for the Macintosh Plus—lowered the bar for entry, speeding up the design process and allowing for more complex layouts and a new wave of typeface design. Debates raged between Modernists, who were skeptical of the emerging aesthetics, and Postmodernists, who were interested in pushing the limits of this new technology, and a publishing ecosystem grew up around the conversations between the two.

This was the beginning of the design media landscape as we know it today. In 1990, Rick Poynor founded *Eye* magazine, which quickly established itself as the industry's home base for journalism, criticism, and trendspotting. *Eye*, along with *Emigre*, the San Francisco Bay Area–based avant-garde magazine emerging from the eponymous type foundry run by Rudy VanderLans and Zuzana Licko, quickly became the platforms for serious design writing and spirited debates. Around the same time, magazines like *Print* and *I.D.* began publishing critical pieces on graphic design, as were the handful of academic journals dedicated to design.

In 1994, designers Michael Bierut and William Drenttel, along with design writer and historian Steven Heller, published the first book in the Looking Closer series, an anthology of the best recent design writing that, over the next decade, would span five volumes. But still, as great as these initiatives were (and are), they were largely platforms made by

2 Michael Rock and Rick Poynor, "What Is This Thing Called Graphic Design Criticism?," *Eye* 4, no. 16 (Spring 1995), https://www.eyemagazine.com/feature/article/what-is-this-thing-called-graphic-design-criticism.

Read Poynor on the "First Things First" manifesto on page 56.

designers for designers. In the midst of this discourse, the term "design criticism" gained popularity, as designer-writers were hopeful that a larger discourse around graphic design could exist beyond the profession. Perhaps one day, every newspaper would hire a design critic, like they had art, architecture, film, and food critics.

In a conversation in *Eye* magazine in 1995, Rick Poynor*and Michael Rock sought to capture the zeitgeist and put a stake in the ground for new ways of talking about design. "We are perhaps the first generation of writers who consider themselves, as a form of self-definition, to be graphic design critics," Rock said. "And that sense of being at the beginning of something is extremely liberating."[2] The two went on to discuss the relationship between design and writing, and what type of design criticism they wanted to see more of. Where Poynor articulated a type of "journalistic criticism" that frames a designer or designed object in a larger context, Rock was interested in applying cultural criticism, like literary theory or semiotics, to design writing. There was an optimism in their conversation: designers wanted to be understood, and it seemed they were on the right path toward acquiring cultural significance.

Yet when the two reconvened nearly twenty years later for a follow-up conversation, published in Rock's 2013 monograph *Multiple Signatures*, much of that bright-eyed optimism was absent. In the preceding two decades, magazines like *I.D.* and *Print* had shut down, to be replaced by design blogs like *Design Observer* and *SpeakUp*, which made design writing more accessible—and which then had been replaced in turn by social media, which distributed the conversation across a yet wider group of people. "I don't think we need too many more vague academic 'calls' for criticism," Poynor said. "We need action. We need a lot more criticism and places to disseminate it."[3] Poynor's language here is reminiscent of Massimo Vignelli's, who, when asked to write a foreword to the 1983 *Graphis Annual*, used his space to issue a call for a more rigorous design criticism:

> It is time that theoretical issues be expressed and debated to provide a forum of intellectual tension out of which meanings spring to life. Pretty pictures can no longer lead the way in which our visual environment should be shaped. It is time to debate, to probe the values, to examine the theories that are part of our heritage and to verify their validity to express our times. It is time for the word to be heard. It is time for Words of Wisdom.[4]

In fact, there's never been much optimism around design criticism (with Poynor and Rock's early conversation a clear outlier) given the seemingly perennial calls like Vignelli's for more of it, with more rigor. For example, Steven Heller wrote in AIGA's *The Journal* in 1993: "A profession that cannot support professional critics is in danger of perpetually noodling its navel."[5] And Poynor again in 2005, in a post on *Design Observer* called "Where Are the Design Critics?": "How are designers going to become critical in any serious way if they are not exposed to sustained critical thinking about design in the form of ambitious, intellectually penetrating criticism?"[6] In 2012, Alexandra Lange wrote in *Print* magazine, "If design—graphic, product, interaction—needs criticism to make it whole and mature, it seems clear we aren't there yet."[7] Khoi Vinh wrote in *Fast Company* in 2018, "Design as an industry has never been able to support a truly robust class of

3 Michael Rock, "What Is This Thing Called Design Criticism?," in *Multiple Signatures: On Designers, Authors, Readers and Users*, ed. Michael Rock (New York: Rizzoli, 2013), 235.

4 Massimo Vignelli, "Call for Criticism" 1983), in *Looking Closer 3*, ed. Michael Bierut, Jessica Helfand, Steven Heller, and Rick Poynor (New York: Allworth Press, 1999), 273.

5 Steven Heller, "Criticizing Criticism: Too Little and Too Much" (1993), *Eye on Design*, November 18, 2014, https://eyeondesign.aiga.org/criticizing-criticism-too-little-and-too-much/.

6 Rick Poynor, "Where Are the Design Critics?," *Design Observer*, September 25, 2005, https://designobserver.com/article.php?id=3767.

7 Alexandra Lange, "An Anatomy of Uncriticism," *Print*, January 5, 2012, https://www.printmag.com/featured/an-anatomy-of-uncriticism/.

8 Khoi Vinh, "Design Discourse Is in a State of Arrested Development," *Fast Company*, January 29, 2018, https://www.fastcompany.com/90155005/design-discourse-is-in-a-state-of-arrested-development.

9 Rock and Poynor, "What Is This Thing Called Graphic Design Criticism?"

10 Reggie Ugwu, "SiriusXM Is Buying '99% Invisible,' and Street Cred in Podcasting," *New York Times*, April 26, 2021, https://www.nytimes.com/2021/04/26/arts/siriusxm-99-invisible-roman-mars.html.

professional journalists and critics....Even the idea of someone spending their days writing reviews of brand identities, design systems, app experiences, and the design of new products seems far-fetched."[8] And when in 2022, I spoke to Cliff Kuang, the cofounder and former editor of *Fast Company*'s *Co.Design*, he told me: "I thought we were on the verge of a new generation of design critics where everyone would be covering design. It still hasn't happened."

And yet, more people are talking about graphic design today than ever before. "While we might not recognize it as such, design criticism is everywhere, underpinning all institutional activity—design education, history, publishing, and professional associations," Rock responded to Poynor back in 1995. "The selection, description and reproduction of designed artefacts in books and magazines, for instance, is the work of theory."[9] Indeed, design criticism as a narrow term never developed into the field the two discussed on that day, but if we accept Rock's expansive definition, then we can find writing about design everywhere, even when it isn't called design writing. When a company rebrands, discussions about the new look push the company into Twitter's trending topics and are covered by publications from *Wired* and *Fast Company* to the *New York Times* and *The Economist*.

Design media, it turns out, is a big business. "When we started *Co.Design*, a third of *Fast Company*'s traffic was design stories," Kuang told me. The popular design-centric podcast *99% Invisible* was purchased by SiriusXM in 2021 for what the *New York Times* reported was at least a million-dollar deal.[10] During the same year, *Dezeen*, the popular design media platform, was purchased by a Danish media

company for an undisclosed sum. In 2017 and
again in 2019, design was given the chef's-table
treatment with *Abstract: The Art of Design*, a glossy
Netflix docuseries on celebrity designers.

So why *doesn't* every major newspaper have
a design critic? Why did design criticism per se never
catch on? Why do designers still feel like their work is
misunderstood? "This kind of discourse is harkening
back to some idealized, romantic notion of a media
landscape where people would read a newspaper
from front to back in material form or where there
is a central public conversation," Alice Twemlow,
a design writer and a design lecturer at the Royal
Academy of Art, the Hague, told me. "This is a kind
of lazy nostalgia." She says training her students
at the School of Visual Arts' Design Criticism MFA
program—one that she cofounded and chaired
before moving to the Hague—for possible jobs as
critics at newspapers was a "fool's errand." (A few
years ago, SVA changed the name of the program
from simply Design Criticism to the more expansive
Design Research, Writing and Criticism, acknowledging the evolving platforms for discussing design.)

When I asked Michael Rock why we continue
to call for more criticism almost thirty years after his
conversation with Poynor, he also described a veneer
of nostalgia. "I wonder if part of these calls is actually
a feeling of loss," he said, "of losing a center where
we had something that we could point to and say 'this
is our criticism.'" Rock doesn't think this loss is simply about a changing media landscape, however, but
rather about the changing nature of graphic design
itself: "I see graphic design as something that began
in the 1920s and died in 2008. It doesn't exist anymore. And the reason it doesn't exist is because it's
completely infiltrated everything."

23

11 Tim Brown, "Design Thinking," *Harvard Business Review*, June 2008, https://hbr.org/2008/06/design-thinking.

12 Jonah Lehrer, "Steve Jobs: 'Technology Alone Is Not Enough,'" *New Yorker*, October 7, 2011, https://www.newyorker.com/news/news-desk/steve-jobs-technology-alone-is-not-enough.

When design is written about today, it's often under the wider fields of "technology" or "culture" or even "branding." And as tech journalists ever more frequently cover user-interface changes coming out of Silicon Valley, the roles of designers in these complex systems become increasingly blurry. For the last few years, the *New York Times Magazine* combined what had previously been separate thematic issues into an annual "Technology and Design Issue." Visual culture, from TikTok to memes to viral videos to Instagram aesthetics, is a popular topic for journalists to cover.

Branding, too, has become a field of study interesting not just to designers but to marketers, business leaders, and social media managers, and spans not just visual design but storytelling, editorial, and advertising. When Tim Brown wrote about design thinking—another text that helped catapult design into the larger culture—he published it in the *Harvard Business Review*![11] "This is the problem with that word 'design,'" Kuang told me. "Design covers interiors and furniture and apps and products. They're all different concerns with different problems, but they are all responses to the culture."

Here lies the paradox of design media. To be taken seriously, then, is not to define graphic design as something separate, but to move it beyond the confines of the discipline. Graphic design is a profession that exists at the intersections, a bridge that connects many fields and professions. Design serves as a meeting point between culture and commerce, or, as Walter Gropius described it at the Bauhaus, between art and technology. Steve Jobs borrowed this when he described Apple as the "intersection of technology and liberal arts."[12] Rock marks the end of graphic design in 2008, coinciding with the rise of the iPhone. Like the Macintosh before it, the iPhone radically scrambled what we mean when we talk about design. Here was a tool for creation, distribution, and consumption, all in a single device that everyone could access.

13 Victor Papanek, *Design for the Real World* (Toronto: Bantam Books, 1971), 23.

"I'm becoming less and less dogmatic about holding on to this label of design," Twemlow told me. "When I first started working at the Royal Academy of Art, I felt like an apologist for design. I kept going on and on about it. But I've stopped doing that so much. I just let it be without all these walls and forts built up around it." This expansion of design, then, is not one of colonization—of design moving in and taking over—but of democratization, of shifting power from the professional to the amateur.

"That rhetoric—it's very much about founding, about establishing, about earning respect," Twemlow adds regarding Vignelli's call for criticism. "It's about the differences between design and art, or design and whatever. I think we're a long way past that now." When I asked Rock how he was feeling about the design discourse today, he was decidedly more optimistic. "What I missed then is this expansion of design into all these different fields," he said. "And with that comes tons of writing that we don't always consider design writing."

"Any attempt to separate design, to make it a thing-by-itself," Victor Papanek wrote in *Design for the Real World* (1971), "runs counter to its inherent value as the underlying matrix of life."[13] As the world increasingly runs on visuals, writers of all kinds have become more comfortable writing about branding and typography, user interface and style, in the business pages and the fashion magazines, in major newspapers and technology journals. As Twemlow said to me, putting design in its own section of the newspaper was always self-defeating in terms of fostering a wider understanding of design. "This has been the problem all along," she said, "namely, treating design as this arcane, esoteric thing." Graphic design writing, then, is indeed everywhere, just as graphic design is everywhere. We just might not recognize it because we don't even recognize design.

Personal Branding Just Got a Lot More Branded

by Liz Stinson

ORIGINALLY PUBLISHED JANUARY 28, 2021

There was a time when branding felt relegated to the world of products and services. Cereal had branding, banks had branding, start-ups had branding. But people? Not so much. Of course, over the last decade that's changed, as social media gave humans the opportunity to market themselves as living, breathing commodities. Suddenly, people were making money being a version of themselves that could be packaged and sold in the burgeoning influencer economy. In the influencer era, the notion of a personal brand—not a new concept by any means—has become a lot more branded. So much so that humans now design and sell merchandise based off of their online personas.

This is the moment we found ourselves in when this story first ran in 2021. Chef influencer Molly Baz had recently released a line of products she called Molly Merch, designed with her own personal visual brand in mind. It struck me as a subtle but important shift: from the early days of personal branding, when influencers were simply a marketing tool for companies looking to reach a particular demographic, to a moment when influencers themselves became direct-to-consumer goods. Fast forward to today, and this trend has only accelerated. No longer is the idea of branded personhood shocking or even novel. It's almost nonnegotiable for anyone trying to build a business.

———

ae Sal" started with a video. It was 2018, and Molly Baz's husband had gifted her a pair of Nike sneakers customized with a misspelled abbreviation of the *Bon Appetit* chef's favorite food—Caesar salad. In the clip, Baz is seen standing in *Bon Appetit*'s airy downtown New York City test kitchen, showing off a pair of black sneakers featuring blocky text reading "CEA SAL" printed across the shoes' tongues.

"Why?" one of Baz's colleagues deadpanned.

"Because," Baz replied, pointing a shoe in his direction, "'cae sal' is one of my favorite dishes in the world."

For those not among the 2.1 million people who have watched the video, "cae sal" (pronounced see-sal) is one of Baz's most famous Molly-isms, the cheerful abbreviations the chef sprinkles into her videos and Instagram captions. Other gastronomical diminutives include "sandos" (sandwiches) "pepp" (pepper) and "cotty-c" (cottage cheese). Since the video aired, "cae sal" has become a cross-platform inside joke for those who know. And a lot of people know.

Back in December, Baz explained to me over Zoom that "cae sal" was one of the main pillars of Brand Molly that emerged during her time at *Bon Appetit*. "That and the love of my weenie dog over here," she said, nodding to the caramel-colored dachshund lounging on the bed behind her. Two

weeks prior, Baz had released a collection of merchandise dubbed Molly Merch through a website
she set up in preparation for the new phase of her
career. After a tumultuous summer at *Bon Appetit*
where the editor in chief resigned amid a social
media scandal over accusations of unfair treatment
of staff members of color, Baz decided to leave the
magazine to start a paid newsletter called Molly's
Recipe Club.

The first of five merch "drops" Baz had planned
for the year featured a list of quarantine-friendly
loungewear and goods: aprons dyed in saturated
primary colors; tie-dyed sweatshirts and crewnecks
featuring an embroidered logo of her dog, Tuna;
a white pocket T-shirt and baseball cap featuring
"Cae Sal" printed in cobalt. "I'm really looking forward to / kind of nervous about walking down the
street and seeing someone rocking a 'Cae Sal' tee,"
she said. "I think it's going to be a moment for me."

Baz started Molly Merch as a way to drum up
interest around her upcoming cookbook, *Cook
This Book*, but it has quickly become its own successful revenue stream. With the help of merch company
Jane Music Group and her more than six hundred
thousand Instagram followers, Baz's first drop was as
successful as some of the bigger names Jane Music
Group has worked with, including Kendrick Lamar
and Jaden Smith. "Molly sold comparable units
despite her following being smaller," said Jane Music
Group founder Lea Sindija, who didn't want to give
exact numbers on Baz's sales. "It shows how engaged
her fan base is." The top seller from the first collection was the tie-dyed crewneck featuring Tuna,
which has become Baz's de facto logo. "We found
out that people are super obsessed with Tuna,"
Sindija said. "But we already kind of knew that."

Shirt designed for Molly Baz's Molly Merch drop in 2021. Typography and illustration by the French studio Violaine et Jérémy.

> "
> It's the logical last step in the trajectory of humans-as-branding: the personal brand becomes a regular brand, full circle.
> "

Many of the first collection's design details were pulled directly from the splashy, colorful graphics found in her cookbook, designed by French studio Violaine et Jérémy. Baz's merch typography (the playfully geometric Dida, a typeface favored among other culinary stars) echoes the cobalt blue found on the cookbook's cover. The designers say they wanted to create something "bold and playful," but that they were branding Molly's cookbook, not her. "In our opinion, you never brand a person; you always brand a skill, a savoir-faire," they said. "Molly doesn't brand herself as a person—she brands her cooking skill, her cooking style. It's really important to detach your very self from your brand. This is an intellectual pirouette which we think is essential for the well-being of the person."

Beyond aprons, Baz is using the red, blue, and yellow color palette on her website, in her newsletter, and on custom Instagram backgrounds for announcing big projects. The merch is but one component of a coordinated visual identity that Baz can deploy across the different branches of her expanding business. "I felt like there was a pretty established 'Molly brand' in terms of what it stands for when I left *BA*, but there wasn't an established brand as far as what it looks like," she said. "I've been spending a lot of time focusing on establishing a singular visual brand."

In the early days of social media, the way we presented ourselves online didn't require a visual distillation of brand attributes. Personal brands were largely intangible, buoyed by two-dimensional avatars lurking in the corners of social apps and websites. For the most talented, the most vocal, or the most shameless, a personal brand was simply a by-product of making and sharing work. That's changing as the business around how creators make money evolves. While personal brands used to be a way to garner enough cultural capital to net a paid gig at a magazine or company, creators quickly realized that they didn't need established companies to mediate their content, so they took to the platforms to monetize themselves through clicks, ad revenue, and brand partnerships. Today, influencers view themselves as entrepreneurs, and their personas as a direct-to-consumer good that can take a multitude of forms. It's the logical last step in the trajectory of humans-as-branding: the personal brand becomes a regular brand, full circle.

Because social media has enabled the persona to become a viable and lucrative business, influencers now embrace the same tools that corporations and technology start-ups use to communicate their messages to mass audiences. Creating a cohesive visual identity allows a person to divide their brand into physical, sellable components. The consequence of that is infinite ways to sell yourself directly to the people who want to buy your product—i.e., you.

If there was ever hesitancy to think of one's personality as a tangible, marketable good, that sentiment has now totally disappeared, as individuals with large online followings sell merch emblazoned with their names, faces, and signature catchphrases. For a certain strata of young influencers, selling a sweatshirt with their name printed on the arm of a hoodie can be just as lucrative as the advertising revenue they receive from getting millions of eyeballs on a YouTube video. Creators like YouTube star David Dobrik have said that the merchandise they sell through online shops composes the majority of their income.[14] The rise in persona merch is aided by companies like Fanjoy and Killer Merch, which provide the infrastructure for creators to design, manufacture, and sell merch with little thought or effort.

The desire to physically commoditize one's persona is part of a long history of businesses using goods as a form of brand extension. It's garden-variety entrepreneurship, explains Tom Peters, an author and consultant who popularized the term "personal branding" back in the late 1990s with an article in *Fast Company* called "The Brand Called You."[15] "Welcome to social media, where everybody is selling their damn name," he says.

And yet, with her merch, Baz has seemingly broken an unspoken rule of self-promotion for the generation of middle-millennials conditioned to toe the delicate line between necessary self-aggrandizing and applauded humility: Don't try too hard. A little

14 Amanda Perelli, "Inside Fanjoy Influencer Merchandise Business: David Dobrik, Jake Paul," *Business Insider*, April 9, 2020, https://www.businessinsider.com/inside-fanjoy-influencer-merchandise-business-youtube-david-dobrik-jake-paul-2020-4.

15 Tom Peters, "The Brand Called You," *Fast Company*, August 31, 1997, https://www.fastcompany.com/28905/brand-called-you.

self-deprecation goes a long way. And god forbid you make money off your name, talent, and enthusiasm lest you be considered a sellout. Baz's new venture highlights the paradox of modern personal branding: giving your personal brand an actual brand can feel either savvy or galling. It just depends on whom you ask.

The difference of opinion often breaks along generational lines. "For people in my generation, it does seem a lot more natural because we grew up parallel to all these different trends," said Abby St. Claire, a twenty-three-year-old designer and model living in San Francisco who runs a merch shop where she sells hoodies and T-shirts printed with designs of her own making. St. Claire started selling merch as a way to promote her Meme Friday project, where she posts downer memes on her Instagram Stories. The merch design lightly pokes fun at current streetwear trends that St. Claire describes as "low-fi, high vibe." "It's probably what the cool kids in LA or New York are wearing," she says.

St. Claire has fewer than ten thousand followers on Instagram and has sold upward of fifty pieces of merchandise. It's not enough to make a living, but that's not really the point, she says. St. Claire says she's bought merch from her favorite creators like Twitch star Noel Miller and YouTube comedian Cody Ko as a form of appreciation for the work they make. "They make me laugh all the time, so I'm happy to throw them a couple of bucks to show my support." It's also a matter of classic self-marketing: like its higher-profile cousin, streetwear, wearing personalized merch is a way to signal to others how you want to be seen. "It's the same reason why I think people for a while were reading issues of *Monocle* on the train," said Grace Clarke, a consultant who specializes in brand positioning and growth for Gen Z. "It was such an advertisement for the type of person they were."

The ability to readily articulate and aestheticize one's defining personality traits is a skill distinct to generations that have grown up with the feedback loop of social media, where we experience real-time commentary on what resonates, or not, with those observing us. It's almost like we're living in a never-ending client meeting, where everyone is a stakeholder.

This version of the personal brand is not what Peters had in mind when he wrote his piece for *Fast Company* more than twenty years ago. Peters says that in some ways he wishes he never uttered the phrase "personal branding," as it's become so complicit in the cult of personality that he believes has rotted the minds of many Americans. Peters originally imagined the rise of the personal brand within a large organization; defining who you were as an individual employee was a way to shake off the drone-like anonymity of wearing a badge and a blue button-down.

"The thing that pisses me off about the interpretation of my article is that people have said that 'Brand You' is about marketing yourself," Peters says. "That is absolutely, antithetically not the case. It is about you being perceived as a person of value. It's almost anti-marketing." Taken to its extreme, Peters says, the ability to manufacture a successful personal brand is what enabled someone like Donald Trump to become president. On a more quotidian level, it's what ties so many of us to the social platforms that we claim to despise. It's also what allows us to fulfill the great millennial dream of doing work that we love.

We build our brands across platforms as a necessary evil of living and working online, casting words, podcasts, videos, and newsletters out into the world. In return, success is often directly correlated to follower count. We assess the value of what we create by the number of people who see, share, and comment, and as a result our livelihoods begin to feel irreversibly linked to how we present ourselves to the world.

"
Giving your personal brand an actual brand can feel either savvy or galling. It just depends on whom you ask.
"

At the extreme end of the spectrum, this dynamic produces someone like Chiara Ferragni, the Italian influencer who last fall announced that her personal brand would be going public on the Italian stock market. Selling personal merchandise through Shopify looks like a neighborhood bake sale in comparison, but Clarke believes it's a small but sure step toward a world where individuals exist in their own personality-based universe of profitability. "I think it's the difference between being comfortable with the world we live in right now, where humans are themselves but they sell things, versus this metaverse that I feel like we're barreling toward, which is just like a *Ready Player One* level of simulation," she says.

In many ways we're already there. The Martha Stewarts of the world breached the simulation long ago, albeit on an entirely different level. Running an eponymous lifestyle empire that's sold at Target and that can only be described as "omnimedia" is lumbering and bureaucratic when you look at how the next-gen Martha Stewarts are approaching their brands. (Stewart's approach, we can safely assume, is also much more profitable.) Baz and her contemporaries, by comparison, are not household names in the same way. They are the product of an internet that has splintered stardom into niches, where a smaller but devoted contingent of people care enough about them to walk around with a stranger's dog on their sweatshirt.

Even if the younger generation of chefs, influencers, and creators ultimately aspires to Martha Stewart–level ubiquity, it will inevitably look different in the future. Today, personal brands are more nimble and more immediate. Instead of filtering one's personality through TV and magazines, we get a personality IV injected directly into our brains. This kind of unmediated relationship between the people creating content and the people consuming it requires creators to increasingly give themselves over to an audience: selfies become front-facing prerecorded videos, and videos become live broadcasts. With every brand validation, it gets easier and easier to do.

Once you realize your audience not only tolerates you but wants more of you, selling merchandise doesn't feel so strange. Baz says it took some time to break through a wall of discomfort before she felt like she could accept that people are now just as interested in her as they are in her recipes. Selling merch, posting on Instagram, promoting cookbooks—these are unavoidable tasks on a to-do list when you're your own boss and your own brand. "I don't think you can grow if you're ashamed of promoting yourself," she said. "I try to strike a balance of being real about it and not being...I don't want to be corporate. I'm just a girl who makes yummy food and sells some cool-looking shit."

Three Books That Expand Design History

BRIAR LEVIT

W. E. B. DU BOIS'S DATA PORTRAITS: VISUALIZING BLACK AMERICA
Edited by Whitney Battle-Baptiste and Britt Rusert
2018
—

This book represents an important turning point in how we understand our histories. Most of us think of W. E. B. Du Bois primarily as a civil rights leader—and he was—but he and his collaborators were also responsible for an incredible collection of data visualization about the social status of Black people in Georgia at the turn of the twentieth century. This work has only recently been looked at through the lens of graphic design. Excellent context is included along with visual analysis by designer and educator Silas Munro.

QUEER X DESIGN: 50 YEARS OF SIGNS, SYMBOLS, BANNERS, LOGOS, AND GRAPHIC ART OF LGBTQ
Andy Campbell
2019
—

At the time of this writing, there is simply no other book that covers queer graphic design history at this scale. Campbell covers the classics like the rainbow flag and the pink triangle, but also digs into less iconic designs that are important nevertheless, like guidebooks helping queer folks travel safely (*Bob Damron's Address Book*), infographics showing "gay semiotics," and more.

A HISTORY OF
ARAB GRAPHIC DESIGN
Bahia Shehab and
Haytham Nawar
2020
—

This expansive book explores the
people and events that helped shape
the field of graphic design in the
Arab world. By tracing the history
of graphic design from the nineteenth
century to the late twentieth, the
authors paint a vivid portrait of how
closely tied graphic design has been to
the cultural formations of Arab countries. Filled with more than six hundred
images, the book is as much a visual
history as a written one.

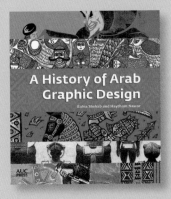

Teaching Design History

by Briar Levit

t has been forty years since the world was introduced to its first survey of graphic design as a discipline—*Meggs' History of Graphic Design*, published in 1983. While other books have emerged as challengers, Philip B. Meggs's book has had a lasting impact on the mythology and curriculum of graphic design. But in recent years, design educators have been activated after a string of events, including an overdue racial reckoning, a harrowing Donald Trump presidency, rising climate crisis warnings, gender dialogues, and a global pandemic. It has led to a new and lively critique of various aspects of the canon happening online and in print. Educators are producing and disseminating new research, while rewriting and reformatting university curricula.

I recently sat down with four graphic design educators to discuss the evolution of graphic design history education as we've witnessed it in our own lifetimes.

Tasheka Arceneaux-Sutton
Associate professor, University of Texas, Austin

Dina Benbrahim
Endowed assistant professor of graphic design, University of Arkansas

Saki Mafundikwa
Founder, Zimbabwe Institute of Vigital Arts

Ramon Tejada
Associate professor, Rhode Island School of Design

16 Sylvia Harris, "Searching for a Black Aesthetic in American Graphic Design" (1986), in *The Education of a Graphic Designer*, ed. Steven Heller (New York: Allworth Press, 2005), 125–29.

BRIAR LEVIT: Did your own education include a design history component?

DINA BENBRAHIM: I went to the University of Florida for grad school. Luckily, I had a professor who was invested in an alternative way of teaching design, but it was more or less still covering the canon and asking us to research overlooked narratives. I didn't realize that I could study Moroccan design until I graduated and left and was like, "Oh, shit, actually I don't know anything about my own country's design."

That's when I started investigating. That's how I started studying Indigenous Amazigh rugs—because I wanted to intersect feminism with the history of my own country. My professor planted the seed.

TASHEKA ARCENEAUX-SUTTON: My undergrad degree was in English. I stumbled upon graphic design later on. I didn't take any design history classes; I actually just bought books and kind of taught myself art history and design history. When I went to grad school at CalArts, a private art institution, there was a design history class that was mandatory. My design history professor was amazing, very knowledgeable, but we did not cover anyone who looked like me—Black people or people of color.

I learned a ton, and because I was the only Black student my first year at CalArts, I began to ask the question: When was the last time they had a Black student in this program—undergraduate or graduate? I also started being interested in the question of: Is there a Black aesthetic in graphic design? When I started doing research, I stumbled across Sylvia Harris's essay "Searching for a Black Aesthetic in American Graphic Design" (1986).[16] I also ran across Ron Eglash's *African Fractals* (1999). Those readings gave me a foundation—they were very eye-opening.

In one project about design genealogy, we had to talk about ten images that influence our design, and when I made my chart, I noticed it had to do with film and literature and books and music that were all directly connected to Black culture and identity. But in art and design, there was nothing. And the only woman on my list—mind you, this was my first year in grad school—was Hannah Höch. I was embarrassed, to be honest, in the beginning, to realize that I couldn't even name one Black designer, and barely any women, let alone women of color. I spent the rest of my time in grad school searching and asking: Where is the Black in graphic design?

SAKI MAFUNDIKWA: In my undergraduate design studies I was just imitating and following and learning and absorbing. There was no graphic design history. But because I was a fine arts major, I took art history classes, and that's where I started to question what I was hearing. The professor used to talk about "primitivism." "African" was "primitive," yada, yada, yada, and then in the same breath, she would say it influenced European art. So one day I raised my hand and I said, "I don't understand how African art is considered primitive and yet influenced European art in a profound way." She was very embarrassed. She said she was sorry and that when she said "primitive," she meant "different." That it wasn't a value judgment. I replied, "So why don't you just say that? Why don't you just say 'different'? I find that very insulting." That was the beginning of my being a rebel.

17 Johanna Drucker and Emily McVarish, *Graphic Design History: A Critical Guide* (Upper Saddle River, NJ: Pearson, 2008).

At the end of my undergraduate studies my teachers said: Apply to the master's program at Yale. And I was like, are you kidding? But you know how fate works. The person who interviewed me was Alvin Eisenman, who was the head of the department and started the master's program in graphic design. He asked me a question that transformed my life. He asked: "Where are you from?" I said, "Zimbabwe." He said, "What language do they speak there?" And I said, "Shona." And he said, "Is it written?" And I'm thinking, this guy is cuckoo because every language is written. He asked, "What are the characters like?" I asked, "You mean A, B, C, D?" "No, no, no, no. I've heard that there are African societies that have invented writing systems." I said, "Really?" In Africa, we were taught about Egypt and hieroglyphics. But Blacks from sub-Saharan Africa were the ones who invented writing systems. We had never heard that. And I remember thinking, if I get accepted into this program, that's gonna be my thesis. And the rest, as they say, is history.

RAMON TEJADA: I did not take a formal graphic design history class until grad school at Otis. We were given *Graphic Design History: A Critical Guide* (2008), and I will forever say, it's the driest, most boring thing I've ever read.[17] I know that's really offensive to a lot of people, but we gotta keep it real. There was nothing in there that really spoke to me.

During that class in grad school, I read, I took part in it. It was great—great conversation about the same three people. Afterward, I realized that almost 90 percent of the books that I had in graphic design, the first chapters all covered the same story. So you could really write that story in one essay and be done. After grad school I encountered Sylvia Harris's essay

"Searching for a Black Aesthetic in American Graphic Design," and I encountered Saki's book *Afrikan Alphabets* (2004) in the library.[18] And I'm like, what is this? What happened? Wait a minute!

18 Saki Mafundikwa, *Afrikan Alphabets: The Story of Writing in Africa* (West New York, NJ: Mark Batty, 2004).

LEVIT: How has identity been crucial in driving your research and teaching?

BENBRAHIM: I grew up with the mentality that everything from Europe was better than what we have. Although the Moroccan school of Casablanca in 1965 looked away from the model of the Bauhaus and toward Africa to teach works that were within the country and beyond—it wasn't public to me. When I took the design history course, I never thought about studying Morocco itself. I thought about where the gap was. I didn't see women, so it was more the feminist aspect of it than actually going back to my roots. It took me a while to get here and to be like, but wait a second, in Morocco I was surrounded by typography my entire life. It was always there. There was geometry everywhere. Look at the tiles—look at, just, all of it. Colonization is really tricky, because it's not only in the land, but also in the mind and the heart.

TEJADA: I think it's amazing to be sitting here talking with all of you about this, because when I was in school fifteen years ago, there was no language around this. I grew up in New York City. You can't walk around New York City without hitting a person of color from some other place. I think finding the space to realize that where you're coming from is important, and that's what makes you a designer. I could learn everything I want from a book about Switzerland and Germany and the Netherlands, but I have no idea about it. That's not where I came from.

45

I came from a culture that's loud and colorful. It's not organized the same way.

The danger, for me, is resisting the temptation to plug it into the structure that I was taught. Because it's very easy in graphic design for us to go right back to the stuff we learned and plug our stuff into it. In that sense, you're educating yourself all over, which is hard to do as we get older.

LEVIT: In the 1990s there was some writing and discussion that attempted to tackle issues of gender bias, heroes, and form over context. But the status quo seemed to stand its ground. These topics have clearly returned, however, and it feels like this time we're at a tipping point of change in thinking around these issues. Why do you think that is?

MAFUNDIKWA: Because people like W. E. B. Du Bois and the book *Data Portraits: Visualizing Black America* (2018) are being accepted by the mainstream as bona fide. And when I look in *The Black Book* (1974) by Toni Morrison, I see the graphic design that was supposed to be in the design history books for us.

I have come up with a term: "decolonize decolonization." We can't let the colonizers tell us or lead the clarion call for decolonization. There's something wrong about that. That idea came to me during a conversation with Sadie Red Wing. When I talk to her, it's a very different conversation than one I would ever have with you, Briar. That's just the truth. There are things that Sadie and I understand that we don't have to explain to each other. What Dina says about her realization that design was always there in Morocco—it's the same thing throughout Africa. It's the same thing in Latin America. Design is always there. But there's always been this Western value judgment put on everything. Everything in the Western gaze. The minute the gaze changes to something else, then it's questioned.

LEVIT: So is it because there are more faculty and students of color?

MAFUNDIKWA: Yes, yes, yes. I am very happy because some of us now are considered elders. And I accept that with a lot of pride because I've been in the trenches and I've done the work. And now when I see the younger generation coming up and taking up this fight, writing books like *The Black Experience in Design* (2022),* et cetera, you can't imagine how much joy that makes me feel.[19]

BENBRAHIM: Also things get shared across the world because of social media. I think there is more power and visibility because of that. People are aware now that it's unacceptable to teach design, to study design, the way it has been.

TEJADA: For many people, the shit hit the fan in 2020. What we're doing is what we have been taught for so long—that graphic designers react to politics. What we're seeing is that designers need to stop writing the same three books about the same three stories that they've written thirty times.

And now we have a bunch of us, and we're done with that conversation. We're doing our own thing. That's a big difference. It's not just Sylvia Harris or Saki in a conference, who probably did a slew of conferences where you were the only person of color there, right? Now when I sit on a panel and there's twelve of us people of color, I'm like, okay, the melanin is for real. Here we are! You can see people get

19 Anne H. Berry, Kareem Collie, Penina Acayo Laker, Lesley-Ann Noel, Jennifer Rittner, and Kelly Walters, eds., *The Black Experience in Design: Identity, Expression and Reflection* (New York: Simon and Schuster, 2022).

https://aigaeod.co/blackexperience

uncomfortable because we are saying things that fifteen years ago would have made people think we were crazy. *You* thought *we* were navel-gazing, but *you've* been navel-gazing for the last 125 years of this field.

ARCENEAUX-SUTTON: I also want to say that on May 25, 2020, we said, "No more. No more Black bodies." Yet we still didn't have control over our own images. We need control over our voices and how they're presented and represented. We're not gonna let you put us in the back. We're gonna create our own conferences. We're gonna create our own narrative. We're gonna have control over the stories. We're not waiting for anybody else anymore.

BENBRAHIM: Teaching design history from a reversal perspective—depending on who you are and the intersections of your identity, where you're teaching, who is in your classroom—the reactions are different. I think it is because I am in a primarily white institution—my classroom is mostly white, I am the Arab—that I clashed, because it was thought that I was brainwashing the students rather than planting multiple seeds.

MAFUNDIKWA: We now have our new leaders. And one name that has kept coming up this evening is Sylvia Harris. I owe my career to Sylvia, because Sylvia made sure that my voice was heard even before I knew I had a voice. Way before my *Afrikan Alphabets* book came out. She would make sure that if she was organizing an AIGA conference, I had to be there. It was important in terms of putting my name on the roster, so that people knew who Saki Mafundikwa was.

LEVIT: I wonder if studying history in this more plural way also helps us understand our responsibility to help uplift? That is not the case when you're studying your Paul Rands and your Massimo Vignellis.

MAFUNDIKWA: Exactly. That's a very good point.

BENBRAHIM: I think this work is activist work because it is about unlearning and reimagining and collaborating and shifting and dealing with resistance from multiple points of view. At the end of the day, it will make everything richer. If we actually connect other dots, it will just be better.

I have students telling me, "Sorry, this does not apply to my future as a designer. I'm not getting the real history here." I have to explain why learning about more voices will make them a better designer. I think for this to actually work, it has to not only come from people like us, but also be embedded into the entire curriculum. If I'm doing this on my own and nobody else is, it's not helping because it's an isolated case.

TEJADA: But that's where the generation thing is important. As Saki was saying, this is the generation of shifts. A lot of us are the ones who are going to be making curricular decisions very soon.

LEVIT: I was going to ask about the responsibility that you all might feel, knowing we can't teach everything.

BENBRAHIM: There's no point because history is never finished. As long as you're able to plant a seed, and people understand it, then it's a win. If you're

> "
> **This work is activist work because it is about unlearning and reimagining and collaborating and shifting and dealing with resistance from multiple points of view.**
> "

able to go past that resistance, it's a win. It's hard work. It's hard, emotional, intellectual, taxing work.

ARCENEAUX-SUTTON: Another important thing about the multiple narratives is that for some students, it gives them a framework to investigate their own history. When I took design history in grad school, I realized I didn't know anything about Black people in design. I didn't put it on my professors. I, for some reason, took it upon myself. Like, okay, nobody's gonna teach me this. There aren't any books out there. Guess what, Tasheka, you have to do it. You discover the history, you write about it, and you lecture about it, and you share it with other people. In teaching, I'm setting up a framework to get these students to figure out a way to find their own history. It's not our job to tell them everything. We should leave some room for them to do their own discovery.

BENBRAHIM: Maybe our job is just to entice that curiosity and humility.

TEJADA: That's our job as teachers, I think. Period. In all fields, not just graphic design.

LEVIT: I see a lot more accessibility of all of this information. Those things that were written in the 1990s were in academic journals that few subscribed to or could afford. Now they're being published by mainstream publishers, and people who work in the industry are reading them.

ARCENEAUX-SUTTON: And that's important, because if regular people don't have access

and information, then what is the point of writing
a stuffy journal that nobody wants to read?

LEVIT: Podcasts and movies are great ways to talk
about this stuff, too.

TEJADA: Zoom opened up a new portal for a lot of us.
The fact that we can have a conversation right now
with Saki, and Tasheka, and Dina, and myself, and
we're in four different places—I think that's incredible. It's amazing to have these voices in the room.

MAFUNDIKWA: I just want to say, tongue in cheek,
the natives are restless! They don't wanna take it
anymore. We are the natives and we are tired of that
tired old narrative. Ramon, we are going to create our
own mythology. And that's actually a quote by Rumi:
"Don't believe in things that man tells you. Create
your own mythology." I used to end my lectures with
that quote, and I think we can end this discussion
on that note. We are doing it.

Challenging Histories

MADELEINE MORLEY

As journalists, it's easy to take the path most traveled when writing a story on design history. Publicists touting the latest museum shows and new monographs reach out with prepackaged material. Design stars from the past are eloquent and easy to reach, not to mention well practiced in the art of the interview after years of media experience. And lengthy articles and meaty books are easy to come by when looking into famous graphic design movements from the past. What's harder is to uncover unknown stories—the ones that center marginalized people or call into question the typical definitions of "graphic design."

To write outside of the canon takes investigating. It takes patience. And it takes time. Time that's precious in a world of spinning news cycles, when online publications feel the pressure to publish quickly, for more clicks and fresh eyes. This is one of many reasons why challenging the status quo—and writing alternative design histories—is so difficult in the journalistic space.

But over the years at *Eye on Design*, we've managed to carve out quiet moments when we could uncover lesser-known figures and movements, follow mysterious leads, wait patiently for sources to call us back, and dig in dusty archives.

The following images and their corresponding stories relate to articles we've published over the years, which attempted to go against the grain of traditional graphic design history and its storytelling conventions.

It took designer and researcher Jerome Harris many months to track down PHASE 2 for an interview—partly because we couldn't source his birth name, given that keeping identity separated from tags is vital for protecting aerosol artists. In the 1970s, the young artist from the Bronx became known as one of the best aerosol writers in the city. He was infamous for his Letraset graphic fliers promoting local rap nights. PHASE 2's layouts helped to define the aesthetics of the hip-hop movement. Yet while hip-hop

52

PHASE 2, flyer for the Ecstasy Garage Disco, New York, 1980.

right:
Söre Popitz, advertisement
for Thügina, 1925/1933. Proof
on paper, 15 × 12.7 cm.

below:
Mari Tepper, *Hallelujah
the Pill*, 1967.

evolved from a small music scene of Black youth in the Bronx to the worldwide phenomenon it is today, his influential designs never quite made it into the annals of design history. In a long-form interview, Harris charted the origins of PHASE 2's "Funky Nous Deco" aesthetic.
https://aigaeod.co/phase2

In histories of the Bauhaus, it's often said that there were no women advertising designers that emerged from the school, as women were largely encouraged to pursue weaving instead. But as with most things, it's just a question of framing. Advertising designer and graphic artist Söre Popitz studied at the Bauhaus for a brief stint. She is often left out of its history since she was only there for one semester, yet her abstracted, geometric designs unmistakably bear the influence of the school and its masters. There are only a few scraps left in Popitz's archive, as her studio was destroyed during the bombing of Leipzig, Germany. Had she stayed at the Bauhaus, her work would have been preserved within the institution's archive—but she would have also likely been ushered into the weaving workshop and never pursued graphics in the first place.
https://aigaeod.co/sorepopitz

Psychedelic design, with its oozing patterns, Day-Glo ink, and swinging-1960s illustrations, is typically thought of as a maledominated scene. For a story on women at the margins of the movement, we uncovered the patriarchal undertones of the San Francisco 1960s design world, speaking with women who produced graphics at the time but were dissuaded from pursuing a career in the field. For Mari Tepper, who designed promotional material for Janis Joplin's Big Brother and the Holding Company and the Grateful Dead as a sixteen-year-old, it was her then-boyfriend who snuffed out her dream to pursue poster design (he threatened to break up with her if she didn't throw away her paints). Her celebratory poster about birth control pills for the American Newsrepeat Company sold more than sixty thousand copies, but she was never paid. In our interview, she noted that those who reaped the historical and financial benefits from the period's infamous graphic art were mostly the "straight white men" of the scene. But instead of feeling embittered, she became "politicized."
https://aigaeod.co/psychedelia

The Evolving Legacy of Ken Garland's "First Things First" Manifesto

by Rick Poynor

ORIGINALLY PUBLISHED AUGUST 12, 2021

I have always been fascinated by manifestos dealing with art and society, though they had become
unfashionable by the 1980s and 1990s, when I was
young: too much twentieth-century disillusion!
From the moment I learned about Ken Garland's
self-published "First Things First," it gripped me—
and I reprinted it in *Eye* magazine, which I edited
at the time. *Adbusters* saw the text, reprinted it
in their own pages, and then decided to rewrite it.
I was delighted to get involved in the campaign.
In the buildup to FTF 2000's international launch,
I collected many related documents, and I continued
on as the unofficial FTF archivist in the years after
publication. It was my hope that a high-powered
researcher would come calling one day (that offer
still stands).

I admit to mixed feelings when Cole Peters's
third version appeared online in 2014. His text zeroed
in on web design, which was a new critique, but
was the reboot entirely necessary, I wondered?
The appearance of a fourth version of FTF in 2020
obliged me to reassess that earlier reaction. The
manifesto's perpetual return was a tribute to the
continuing—indeed, increasing—relevance of its
central critique. New generations of designers clearly
found FTF meaningful as legacy, statement, and
rallying point, and it is entirely right that FTF should
be updated as circumstances change. In the teeth
of our complex global crisis, who can seriously reject
the latest iteration? I wrote my essay to tell the story
of FTF, explore the thinking behind the four versions,
and lend the evolving text my support.

Manifestos no longer look dated, embarrassing, or irrelevant. These distilled texts have the
potential to disturb the status quo, provoke vital

discussions—especially in education—and remind us of what needs to be done. They are vital expressions of a collective will for change.

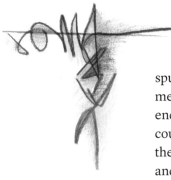

he late Ken Garland's "First Things First" manifesto, written in 1963 on the spur of the moment during a public meeting, has become a tradition of enduring protest that its originator could never have predicted. Last year, the fourth version of the text arrived, and it's the most urgent and powerful iteration to date. In the nearly sixty years since Garland self-published his broadside, the stakes for society and design have spiraled skyward. Despite the British designer's proud self-declaration as a socialist, the politics of the original were always fuzzy. In the latest FTF, the critique of the damage wrought by the excesses of capitalism—which was merely implicit in the first version—is fully articulated. That makes the manifesto more challenging and potentially more divisive than ever. It asks designers to consider which side of the argument they are on.

Garland's FTF, cosigned by twenty-one colleagues, including some photographers, calls for a "reversal of priorities" among graphic designers. It proposes that less design effort should go into advertising—1960s consumer society was booming—and more should go into "worthwhile purposes" such as "signs for streets and buildings, books and periodicals, catalogs, instruction manuals, industrial photography, educational aids, films, television

A manifesto

We, the undersigned, are graphic designers, photographers and students who have been brought up in a world in which the techniques and apparatus of advertising have persistently been presented to us as the most lucrative, effective and desirable means of using our talents. We have been bombarded with publications devoted to this belief, applauding the work of those who have flogged their skill and imagination to sell such things as:

cat food, stomach powders, detergent, hair restorer, striped toothpaste, aftershave lotion, beforeshave lotion, slimming diets, fattening diets, deodorants, fizzy water, cigarettes, roll-ons, pull-ons and slip-ons.

By far the greatest time and effort of those working in the advertising industry are wasted on these trivial purposes, which contribute little or nothing to our national prosperity.

In common with an increasing number of the general public, we have reached a saturation point at which the high pitched scream of consumer selling is no more than sheer noise. We think that there are other things more worth using our skill and experience on. There are signs for streets and buildings, books and periodicals, catalogues, instructional manuals, industrial photography, educational aids, films, television features, scientific and industrial publications and all the other media through which we promote our trade, our education, our culture and our greater awareness of the world.

We do not advocate the abolition of high pressure consumer advertising: this is not feasible. Nor do we want to take any of the fun out of life. But we are proposing a reversal of priorities in favour of the more useful and more lasting forms of communication. We hope that our

society will tire of gimmick merchants, status salesmen and hidden persuaders, and that the prior call on our skills will be for worthwhile purposes. With this in mind, we propose to share our experience and opinions, and to make them available to colleagues, students and others who may be interested.

Edward Wright
Geoffrey White
William Slack
Caroline Rawlence
Ian McLaren
Sam Lambert
Ivor Kamlish
Gerald Jones
Bernard Higton
Brian Grimbly
John Garner
Ken Garland
Anthony Froshaug
Robin Fior
Germano Facetti
Ivan Dodd
Harriet Crowder
Anthony Clift
Gerry Cinamon
Robert Chapman
Ray Carpenter
Ken Briggs

Published by Ken Garland.
Printed by Goodwin Press Ltd. London N4

Ken Garland, "First Things First," 1964.

features, science and industrial publications."
Ian McLaren, the only surviving signatory I could find, had been an intern at an advertising agency as a design student and hated it because the opportunities for designers there were so limited. When Garland offered him the chance to sign FTF, he agreed. "It was more a feeling that it was just 'the right thing to do,'" he says today. "In my case it was more a reaction to a frustration. My political philosophy was pretty hazy then."

It took thirty-five years for the second version, "First Things First 2000," to appear, in fall 1999. Kalle Lasn of *Adbusters* had seen the original in *Eye* magazine and reprinted it. This led to a plan to create an updated version written by *Adbusters* with input

FIRST

The *First Things First* manifesto was initially published in January, 1964. This call-to-arms proclaimed the sentiments of many creatives whose talents were quickly being mulched by the machinery of advertising agencies. Thirty-four years and three reprints later, *First Things First* has become more, rather than less relevant.

"The basis of [this] manifesto was to emphasize what we consider the false priority in spending," stresses participant Ken Garland, "but we also wanted to encourage students, designers and photographers to think about the opportunities for graphic design and photography outside advertising."

THINGS FIRST

Chris Dixon, "First Things First 1964," *Adbusters*, no. 23 (Autumn 1998).

A Manifesto

We, the undersigned, are graphic designers, photographers and students who have been brought up in a world in which the techniques and apparatus of advertising have persistently been presented to us as the most lucrative, effective and desirable means of using our talents. We have been bombarded with publications devoted to this belief, applauding the work of those who have flogged their skill and imagination to sell such things as: *Cat food, stomach powders, detergent, hair restorer, striped toothpaste, aftershave lotion, beforeshave lotion, slimming diets, fattening diets, deodorants, fizzy water, cigarettes, roll-ons, pull-ons, and slip-ons.* By far the greatest time and effort of those working in the advertising industry are wasted on these trivial purposes, which contribute little or nothing to our national prosperity.

In common with an increasing number of the general public, we have reached a saturation point at which the high pitched stream of consumer selling is no more than sheer noise. We think that there are other things more worth using our skill and experience on. There are signs for streets and buildings, books and periodicals, catalogues, instructional manuals, industrial photography, educational aids, films, television features, scientific and industrial publications and all the other media through which we promote our trade, our education, our culture and our greater awareness of the world.

We do not advocate the abolition of high pressure consumer advertising: this is not feasible. Nor do we want to take any of the fun out of life. But we are proposing a reversal of priorities in favour of the more useful and lasting forms of communication. We hope that our society will tire of gimmick merchants, status salesmen and hidden persuaders, and that the prior call on our skills will be for worthwhile purposes. With this in mind, we propose to share our experience and opinions, and to make them available to colleagues, students and others who may be interested.

— *From* eye *magazine*

Edward Wright
Geoffrey White
William Slack
Caroline Rawlence
Ian McLaren
Sam Lambert
Ivor Kamlish
Gerald Jones
Bernard Higton
Brian Grimbly
John Garner
Ken Garland
Anthony Froshaug
Robin Fior
Germano Facetti
Ivan Dodd
Harriet Crowder
Anthony Clift
Gerry Cinamon
Robert Chapman
Ray Carpenter
Ken Briggs

from other interested parties (I was one of them). While the original FTF found its way to British television, where Garland read it live on a national news program, its dissemination outside the country was limited at the time. FTF 2000 was conceived from the outset as an international initiative, and it was launched simultaneously in *Adbusters*, AIGA *Journal of Graphic Design*, and *Emigre* in North America, *Eye* and *Blueprint* in Britain, and *Items* in the Netherlands; *Form* magazine in Germany followed later.

Garland visited *Adbusters* in Vancouver and agreed to add his signature to the revised document. Other signatories—making thirty-three total—were approached by *Adbusters*, Rudy VanderLans of *Emigre* magazine, and me. They included some famous names: Milton Glaser, Ellen Lupton, Steven Heller, Erik Spiekermann, and Gert Dumbar of Studio Dumbar in the Netherlands. This was meant to attract attention to the message, and it succeeded, but the alleged hypocrisy of a few signatories caused intense annoyance among some readers. "Isn't it embarrassing to see a handful of self-appointed design practitioners and educators, totally vested in the security of the stock market, privilege, and the tenure system, speak as prophets for such a complicated and complex world?" wrote Dietmar Winkler, director of the School of Art and Design at the University of Illinois, in a reply to *Adbusters*.

The 2000 version had a similar structure to the original, while broadening its target from advertising to marketing and brand development. Its language and argument brandished the fiery worldview *Adbusters* had spent a decade cultivating. By their actions, designers were supporting "a mental environment so saturated with commercial messages that it is changing the very way citizen-consumers speak,

FIRST THINGS FIRST MANIFESTO—2000

We, the undersigned, are graphic designers, art directors, and visual communicators who have been raised in a world in which the techniques and apparatus of advertising have persistently been presented to us as the most lucrative, effective, and desirable use of our talents. Many design teachers and mentors promote this belief; the market rewards it; a tide of books and publications reinforces it. ▪ Encouraged in this direction, designers then apply their skill and imagination to sell dog biscuits, designer coffee, diamonds, detergents, hair gel, cigarettes, credit cards, sneakers, butt toners, light beer, and heavy-duty recreational vehicles. Commercial work has always paid the bills, but many graphic designers have now let it become, in large measure, what graphic designers do. This, in turn, is how the world perceives design. The profession's time and energy are used up manufacturing demand for things that are inessential at best. ▪ Many of us have grown increasingly uncomfortable with this view of design. Designers who devote their efforts primarily to advertising, marketing, and brand development are supporting, and implicitly endorsing, a mental environment so saturated with commercial messages that it is changing the very way citizen-consumers speak, think, feel, respond, and interact. To some extent we are all helping draft a reductive and immeasurably harmful code of public discourse. ▪ There are pursuits more worthy of our problem-solving skills. Unprecedented environmental, social, and cultural crises demand our attention. Many cultural interventions, social marketing campaigns, books, magazines, exhibitions, educational tools, television programs, films, charitable causes, and other information-design projects urgently require our expertise and help. ▪ We propose a reversal of priorities in favor of more useful, lasting, and democratic forms of communication—a mind shift away from product marketing and toward the exploration and production of a new kind of meaning. The scope of debate is shrinking; it must expand. Consumerism is running uncontested; it must be challenged by other perspectives expressed, in part, through the visual languages and resources of design. ▪ In 1964, twenty-two visual communicators signed the original call for our skills to be put to worthwhile use. With the explosive growth of global commercial culture, their message has only grown more urgent. Today, we renew their manifesto in expectation that no more decades will pass before it is taken to heart.

Jonathan Barnbrook, Nick Bell, Andrew Blauvelt, Hans Bockting, Irma Boom, Sheila Levrant de Bretteville, Max Bruinsma, Siân Cook, Linda van Deursen, Chris Dixon, William Drenttel, Gert Dumbar, Simon Esterson, Vince Frost, Ken Garland, Milton Glaser, Jessica Helfand, Steven Heller, Andrew Howard, Tibor Kalman, Jeffery Keedy, Zuzana Licko, Ellen Lupton, Katherine McCoy, Armand Mevis, J. Abbott Miller, Rick Poynor, Lucienne Roberts, Erik Spiekermann, Jan van Toorn, Teal Triggs, Rudy VanderLans, Bob Wilkinson

"First Things First 2000," *AIGA Journal of Graphic Design* 17, no. 2 (1999).

think, feel, respond, and interact." Graphic design had helped to construct "a reductive and immeasurably harmful code of public discourse." Consumerism was "running uncontested" and designers should help to challenge it.

The response was unprecedented. *Adbusters*, *Emigre*, and other magazines published dozens of letters for and against. Pentagram partner Michael Bierut crafted an elaborate visual riposte for *I.D.* magazine, "A Manifesto with Ten Footnotes," which channeled the irritation of many in the industry at being called to account. "It pays to maintain the status quo," VanderLans snapped back in a letter to *I.D.* Many other magazines reprinted and debated FTF 2000, and translations—French, Italian, Spanish, Portuguese, Czech, Polish, Croatian, Slovenian, Norwegian—reached legions of new readers. The World Wide Web was in its infancy and FTF 2000 was devised as a print-based campaign. *Adbusters* posted it online, and it attracted hundreds of extra signatures, including Bierut's. Then they reprinted the manifesto plus the new signatures as a double-sided folding poster designed by Jonathan Barnbrook, a signatory and fervent supporter.

FTF 2000 gave Garland's original a reboot, and the two documents remained visible for years—see, for instance, the book *Looking Closer 4* (2002)—and prompted countless student FTF projects and redesigns. "Every year I introduce FTF and its versions to my design students," says design educator Elizabeth Resnick, who signed FTF 2014 and FTF 2020 online. "It bears repeating with each new class and each new generation of students." Garland became a hero of the design school lecture circuit. FTF 2000's critics demanded to know what had changed as a result of the manifesto, but the point of both documents was to provoke thought and discussion. It was up to individual designers to decide what path to take and how to apply their convictions.

"Both manifestos made a lasting impression on me, and greatly informed the direction of my career in design and technology," says Canadian web designer Cole Peters. In 2014, FTF's fiftieth anniversary, Peters decided to launch a third version focused on design in the digital realm. "Edward Snowden's disclosures, especially those where technology companies were concerned, gave many of us pause," he recalls. "Technology companies had become a huge source of employment for designers and creative technologists in the 2010s. How culpable were we in this machine that was feasting on personal data and surveillance—a machine that was often made to feel chic and essential through design?" In keeping with its aims, FTF 2014 was launched online, and there were no famous names waving the flag this time around. Anyone in sympathy with the manifesto's imperatives could sign, and more than sixteen hundred people seized the opportunity. As before, the text followed Garland's structure and some of his original phrasing, including his wish not to take the fun out of life.

Garland declared FTF 2014 "admirably concise" when Peters asked for his thoughts before the launch, but he didn't feel that it added much to the previous versions. "For myself, I have no wish to engage in any more manifestos," he replied. By that time, Garland was weary of being painted as the ethically driven author of an "anti-advertising" manifesto. "I say: 'Read it again please!' It's not anti-advertising," he told *Eye*, although its progeny, FTF 2000, which he had endorsed, most certainly was. In a 2012 article he titled "Last Things Last," Garland's overriding

> "
> **Climate change and racial justice work are often represented as two different concerns, but in fact they are interlinked issues due to their roots in capitalism.**
> "

20 Ken Garland,
"Last Things Last," *Eye*
21, no. 83 (Summer 2012),
https://www.
eyemagazine.com/
feature/article/last-
things-last.

concern was to express his appreciation for the
clients he had neglected to acknowledge in the
manifesto forty-eight years earlier.[20]

FTF has escaped and outgrown its creator, and
it's possible that it will continue to mutate. FTF 2000
predated full global awareness of the climate crisis,
and systemic racism went unmentioned. Published
online, FTF 2020, the first US version, blasts the
reader with these issues: "Our time and energy are
increasingly used to manufacture demand, to exploit
populations, to extract resources, to fill landfills,
to pollute the air, to promote colonization, and to
propel our planet's sixth mass extinction." The
manifesto responds with a checklist of urgent design
goals, covering the histories and ethics of design,
community-based initiatives, nonexploitative social
relations, nature as a complex system, and recon-
necting design and manufacturing to the Earth
and its people.

"Climate change and racial justice work are often
represented as two different concerns, but in fact
they are interlinked issues due to their roots in capitalism," says Namita Vijay Dharia, one of FTF 2020's
organizers. "They are produced and perpetuated
together, and climate change vulnerability falls on
the backs of racially and ethnically marginalized
populations across the globe. It was important for us
to add the social justice component, as there can be
no solution to climate change without social justice."

Dharia is an architect, and her FTF colleagues,
Marc O'Brien and Ben Gaydos, were educated as
graphic designers. "We knew we needed to broaden
the definition of design for FTF 2020. We recognized
that every design discipline has contributed directly
or indirectly to our climate crisis," says O'Brien.
Why not devise an entirely new manifesto with no

connection to FTF's history? "Publishing a new manifesto would have tossed our hard work into a sea of overcrowded thought pieces and opinions," he says. "There's lots of noise on the internet. Continuing the legacy of FTF meant bringing the history of the manifesto to a new audience with a new call to action."

To date, FTF 2020 has attracted more than seventeen hundred supporters. "A designer should never feel like they are too late to add their name to something this important," notes signatory Rick Griffith of Matter studio in Denver. "As a Black-led, minority-owned, and LGBT+ business, signing this petition felt like an extension of our values in statement form," says Silas Munro of Polymode, a bicoastal studio. The organizers encourage translations, and FTF 2020 is available in twenty-one languages, including Arabic, Hindi, Turkish, and Vietnamese. Designers who want a platform for action can follow a link to climatedesigners.org, founded by O'Brien. The organizers present FTF as a "living document," and supporters have been adding their thoughts in a Google Doc.* An update of the manifesto will follow.

https://aigaeod.co/ftf

"Our goal was to decentralize the process, to open it up to anyone," says Gaydos. "The three of us wrote a manifesto, but with the help of many other sets of eyes, and in dialogue with the previous iterations of 'First Things First.' It's a love letter to, and even a debate with, Ken Garland and many others about what we need to do to change. It's exciting that FTF 2020 is a living document. It can adapt and change just as we are forced to adapt and change if we want to survive."

Designer Face-Off

by Anne Quito

ORIGINALLY PUBLISHED WINTER 2018

In the late 1980s and early 1990s, the global design community had centralized places of conversation (namely magazines and design conferences), but not much in the way of the instantaneous communication we have today. In the years since my essay on Tibor Kalman and Joe Duffy's dustup was published, graphic designers have become more vocal with their criticism. They're not *not* attacking each other per se, but they are hurling daggers at the tech companies, governments, and organizations behind oppressive systems. This wasn't happening in the centralized agoras of the past. For better or worse, our attentions are now divided and our affiliations have diversified.

Still, in recent years, certain squabbles have broken through the noise enough to conjure that same contentious feeling Kalman and Duffy pioneered decades ago. AIGA medalist Cheryl D. Miller, for instance, chose to pick a fight with design legend Milton Glaser on the very day he died. In a LinkedIn post that she later recapped on *Print*'s website, Miller argued that Black designers lost out on important commissions, particularly those reflecting Black culture, because clients gravitated to Glaser.[21] During a 2020 virtual event convened by the IIT Institute of Design, Miller also aired grievances concerning another dead design idol. "Take down the Paul Rand look," she said. "It's my Confederate flag; my Confederate statue."[22] While not everyone agreed with Miller's posthumous firebombs, her essays shone a spotlight on the overlooked legacy of Black graphic designers.

Type designers, too, are done being polite. Many broke their silence when Monotype, the world's largest font seller, acquired the esteemed

21 Cheryl D. Holmes-Miller, "Black Designers: Forward in Action (Part IV)," *Print*, October 15, 2020, https://www. printmag.com/design-news/black-designers-forward-in-action-part-iv/.

22 "The Future Must Be Different from the Past: Embracing an Anti-racist Agenda," IIT Institute of Design, July 3, 2020, https://id.iit.edu/story/the-future-must-be-different-from-the-past-embracing-an-anti-racist-agenda/.

23 Anne Quito, "A Famous Type Foundry's Sale to a PE-Backed Giant Has Rattled the Font Industry," *Quartz*, October 23, 2021, https://qz.com/2068310/what-monotypes-purchase-of-hoeflerco-means-to-font-designers.

24 Kasia Urbaniak, "Salon 26 Friction," panel discussion at the Museum of Modern Art, New York, June 27, 2018, http://momarnd.moma.org/salons/salon-26-friction-2/.

type foundry Hoefler&Co in 2021. While some questioned the scruples of Jonathan Hoefler (no stranger to design drama), others defended his prerogative to steer the business however he pleased. Many font makers voiced concerns about an impending Monotype monopoly—a "kraken eating up the industry," as one designer put it.[23] Ultimately, the sale led to revelations about the economics of making and selling fonts on the internet. Among veteran designers, the matter also sparked an existential discourse about the viable possibilities or "endgame" for their oeuvre, as the prospect of retirement looms.

e live in an extremely conflict-avoidant society—and I don't just mean the nice people," Kasia Urbaniak said recently at a MOMA R&D salon.[24] Urbaniak, who is a dominatrix turned power dynamics coach, could very well have been describing the genial graphic design industry today.

The fact is, public arguments between graphic designers are rare. Compared to pugnacious novelists, catty couturiers, argumentative architects, or even temperamental typographers, graphic designers are an easygoing bunch—at least on the surface. There may be silent wars or a surfeit of snark on social media, but there hasn't been an all-out ideological throwdown between two designers in decades.

The defining duel in US graphic design happened nearly thirty years ago in San Antonio, Texas. Tibor Kalman shocked the polite crowd at the 1989 AIGA Design Conference when he attacked fellow designer Joe Duffy, who was seated in the audience. In his remarks as co-chair of the conference, Kalman summarized the design industry's decline by flashing an advertisement that Duffy and his then-partner Michael Peters took out in the *Wall Street Journal*. Chewing on the ad's proposition—"how two guys with art degrees can do more for your business than

Joe Duffy and Michael Peters, advertisement for the Michael Peters / Duffy Design Groups, *Wall Street Journal*, 1989.

25 Michael Bierut, "1989: Roots of Revolution," *Design Observer*, March 6, 2004, https://designobserver. com/feature/1989-roots- of-revolution/1957.

26 Steven Heller and Martin Fox, "Tibor Kalman vs. Joe Duffy Revisited," *Print*, April 6, 2011, https://www.printmag. com/designer-interviews/ tibor-kalman-vs-joe-duffy- revisited/.

Joe Duffy

Tibor Kalman

a conference room full of MBAS"—Kalman, along with historian Stuart Ewan and British art director Neville Brody, decried how graphic designers were compromising artistic integrity to serve the commercial goals of big corporate clients.

"We're not here to help clients eradicate every-thing of visual interest from the face of the Earth. We're here to make them think about what's danger-ous and unpredictable. We're here to inject art into commerce," said Kalman. "We're here to be bad."

Kalman, who later showcased his peerless skills as a rabble-rouser as founding art director of *Colors* magazine, accepted Duffy's challenge to an impromptu debate. "A hastily-scrawled sign was posted announcing an unscheduled debate: 'TIBOR: YOU AND ME. TODAY. 5:15. BREAKOUT ROOM G. JOE,'" recalled Michael Bierut, writing about the legendary brawl in *Design Observer*. "Tibor had arranged the chairs in a circle. He and Duffy stood in the middle, circling each other like gladiators. It was pure theater, and more memorable for that than for anything that was said."[25]

Steven Heller was summoned to referee. "When I arrived at the mirrored meeting room—a veritable Texas Versailles—there was already a large crowd of onlookers gathered in a predatory circle," he recalled in a 2011 *Print* article. "Tibor pounced on a somewhat dazed-looking Joe....Joe attempted to duck and jab as best he could, but Tibor was in his element."[26]

Sensing that Duffy didn't get the chance to air his side fairly, Heller organized round two at the *Print* magazine headquarters in New York. What emerged was a spirited tournament between two admired designers that stirred the complacent and increas-ingly self-congratulatory industry. "If Duffy and Kalman did not exactly bask in warmth, they did

Tibor Kalman speaking at the 1989 AIGA Awards Dinner.

27 Heller, "Tibor Kalman vs. Joe Duffy Revisited."

28 Moxie Sozo, "Joe Duffy: Reflecting on His Contentious Debate with Tibor Kalman 28 Years Ago," May 2, 2017, https://moxiesozo. com/2017/05/02/ joe-duffy-reflecting-contentious-debate-tibor-kalman-28-years-ago/.

cast a great deal of light," observes Julie Lasky, *Print*'s then associate editor.

"In the end, the one virtue of the debate...was that heretofore unchallenged design practices were not simply taken for granted but viewed from an ethical and moral lens," wrote Heller. "I don't believe there was a clear winner, but I still feel the design field won because the taboo against head-on criticism was busted, perhaps for the first time."[27] Kalman and Duffy ended on a cordial note but never spoke to each other again. In 2017, Colorado-based branding agency Moxie Sozo asked Duffy what his war with Kalman all meant. "The good news is that more and more people are concerned about good design," he told them, "which is great for all of us designers."[28]

The yin-yang concerns of art and commerce were also at the heart of a heated debate between Dutch design legends Wim Crouwel and Jan van Toorn in 1972. Before the recording was transcribed in 2000 and translated into English for a book fifteen years later, the van Toorn vs. Crouwel affair was

29 Wim Crouwel, Jan Van Toorn, Rick Poynor, Frederique Huygen, and Van De, *The Debate: The Legendary Contest of Two Giants of Graphic Design* (New York: Monacelli, 2015), 32.

30 Crouwel et al., *The Debate*, 29.

31 Steven Heller, "Design's Great Debate," *The Atlantic*, March 12, 2015, https://www. theatlantic.com/ entertainment/archive/ 2015/03/designs-great-debate-to-preserve-the-soul-or-professionalism/ 387532/.

a seminal moment in Dutch graphic design history that existed only as a collective memory. Amsterdam's Museum Fodor, which closed in 1993, served as the arena for their duel. In one corner, Crouwel argued that designers should work with "austere rationalism." Heavily influenced by Swiss design, he promoted the use of efficient grids in graphic communication. "I believe that as a designer I must never stand between the message and its recipient," he said. "Many designers are living with the dilemma of wanting to be a visual artist rather than a good graphic designer."[29]

Arguing for the cause of artists, van Toorn asserted that it's a designer's duty to experiment with new forms and infuse each assignment with one's personality. "The acts you perform take place through you, and you are a subjective link," he said. At one point, he even went so far as to blame Crouwel's template mentality for the scourge of cold, corporate-looking design in the Netherlands. "You impose your design on others and level everything. You were at the forefront, and now our country is inundated by waves of trademarks and house styles and everything looks the same," van Toorn said, eliciting cheers from some in the audience.[30]

Monacelli Press immortalized the event in the 2015 book *The Debate: The Legendary Contest of Two Giants of Graphic Design*, intuiting that the decades-old existential face-off echoes the dilemma of many designers today. "Their positions derive from basic questions that designers ask themselves when they start out: Should my ideas, my personality, my philosophy be evident in my work? Or should I just remove as much of my persona as possible and 'follow the brief'? Or is there a way to do both?" Alan Rapp, the book's editor, explained to *The Atlantic*.[31]

32 "Massimo Vignelli vs. Ed Benguiat (Sort Of)," annotated by Julie Lasky, *Design Observer*, September 15, 2010, https://designobserver. com/feature/massimo- vignelli-vs-ed-benguiat- sort-of/15458.

Jan van Toorn and Wim Crouwel, 2007.

Crouwel and van Toorn's dispute is similar to the clash between Massimo Vignelli and *Emigre* cofounders Rudy VanderLans and Zuzana Licko in 1991. Unnerved by the duo's groundbreaking computer-aided experimentations, Vignelli nixed the politesse to defend culture, as he saw it. "That is a national calamity," he said, referring to the "disgraceful" *Emigre* magazine. "It's not a freedom of culture, it's an aberration of culture. One should not confuse freedom with [lack of] responsibility, and that is the problem. They show no responsibil- ity. It's just like freaking out, in a sense," he said in a debate convened by *Print* magazine. The revered Italian master dismissed the upstarts, calling them a "typographic garbage factory."[32]

"He had no clue that more than half the room thought Zuzana and Rudy were more important than he was," says East Carolina University profes- sor Gunnar Swanson, recalling the episode at an AIGA leadership retreat. Debates about style help foster diversity, he explains. "Some arguments

33 Heller, "Design's
Great Debate."

moved people more toward pluralism and away from tribal restrictions—which is good."

Two topics roil designers: ethics and aesthetics. It's not that designers today aren't capable of critical exchange—there's plenty of that on blogs and social media—but what's missing today is "accountability and critical heft to these skirmishes," as Rapp put it.[33]

Pentagram partner Paula Scher says casual criticism hurts design as a whole. At the 2015 Brand New Conference, Scher outlined the dangers of casual logo commentary, in effect casting a side eye on the popular logo forum *UnderConsideration*, which is published by the conference's organizers, Bryony Gomez-Palacio and Armin Vit. Scher didn't call them out by name, but she was emphatic about how the surge of myopic design mockery can make clients nervous and stifle innovation. Scher's challenge was delivered with tempered eloquence, as many critical essays on graphic design tend to be today. Designers will draft manifestos, paint murals, cling to euphemisms, or criticize big corporations before opposing one another. Is the reluctance to spar a signal of urbanity or apathy?

Why are graphic designers today so afraid of discord? Could it be the years of patience-building practice in client service that inclines us toward compromise? Is it the chumminess of design circles that makes personal feuds awkward to sustain? Or is it because online forums and social media, as Scher suggests, become the default places for critical exchange?

What is missing is friction. Without the heat of conflict, well-meaning group initiatives for diversity, gender parity, or ethics could very well remain intellectual propositions. Urbaniak suggests that, ultimately, it's not a panel discussion or a group

> **Compared to pugnacious novelists, catty couturiers, argumentative architects, or even temperamental typographers, graphic designers are an easy-going bunch— at least on the surface.**

proclamation that will lead to progress, but face-to-face dialogue between opposing minds. "It releases imagination and creates a whole new game for everyone else," she says. "I believe that if people learn how to do this relationship in the form of a dyad, then every social interaction is a form of education."

Bauhaus Meets Binary

by LIZ STINSON

ORIGINALLY PUBLISHED WINTER 2018

Code is a tool—a string of numbers, glyphs, and letters that when arranged in a particular order can be wielded like a screwdriver. But code is a visual medium, too, like illustration or sculpting, that in the right hands can create something optically evocative. Poetic, even.

Since the 1960s, artistically inclined computer scientists and scientifically inclined artists and designers have programmed computers to make work that's impossible to craft by human hand alone. For these so-called creative coders, the computer is an interpreter, responsible for translating impossible ideas into visual form; code is a material that can be bent and broken to that vision.

The history of computer-generated art and design begins in research laboratories equipped with high-powered machines, where computer scientists such as Bell Labs' A. Michael Noll and visual artists including Vera Molnár created experimental forms hovering somewhere between art and scientific inquiry. In time, as computers became cheaper and their programming languages less esoteric, even more artists and designers started using the machines to push their respective fields in wildly new directions.

An inflection point for this new medium occurred in the mid-1980s at MIT, where a group of like-minded designers were at work in Muriel Cooper's Visible Language Workshop (VLW). Cooper, who left MIT Press to start the workshop in 1974, was an early believer in the power of programming to transform the field of graphic design. Through the research conducted in her workshop, she inspired a generation of designers to explore the intersection of design and technology, and in the process built a lineage of creative programmers who, to this day, are shaping the fields of interaction design, graphic design, and new media art. This is their story, in their own words.

———————

John Maeda
Vice president of design and artificial intelligence at Microsoft | former director of the Aesthetics + Computation Group (ACG) at MIT Media Lab

—

David Small
Interaction designer | former student in Muriel Cooper's VLW and Maeda's ACG | founder of Small Design Firm

—

Lisa Strausfeld
Information artist | former student in Cooper's VLW | vice president of design at System

https://
eyeondesign.
aiga.org/muriel-
coopers-visions-
of-a-future

In the mid-1980s, Muriel Cooper's Visible Language Workshop* moved from a warehouse on the outskirts of MIT's campus into the I. M. Pei building that housed the MIT Media Lab. The change in location marked an important transformation for the VLW. Armed with some of the best computers in the world, the designers in Cooper's workshop shifted their primary research from printing presses to their new digital tools. Cooper's workshop, while something of an outlier at the tech-focused MIT Media Lab, quickly gained a reputation as a safe space for experimental design. Its proximity to other Media Lab groups attracted science students such as David Small, who joined after completing a degree in cognitive science, and John Maeda, who never formally joined the workshop but was heavily influenced by Cooper and the VLW's work.

JOHN MAEDA: I was on campus, and I saw what Muriel Cooper was doing with her team. She was thinking about how design and publishing could impact computers. She was the one who boldly believed that someday you'd read Helvetica on a computer screen. People would laugh at her because it was a five-by-seven dot-matrix font just blinking at you.

DAVID SMALL: I was an MIT undergraduate studying science. I was into brain science and cognition, or at least I thought I was, but I was always really interested in photography. I had started taking photography classes, and the VLW was across the hall, so I started hanging out more and more and getting interested in what people were doing. When I finished my undergrad work, I thought: what they're doing at the VLW is so much more interesting than what they're doing in cognitive science.

Muriel recognized earlier than anybody that computers were where it was at. She could have continued to be the design director of MIT Press forever, but she was like, no, these computer things that everyone thinks are lame are going to be really interesting.

MAEDA: The VLW was full of designers trying to figure out how to use computers in interesting ways. I came from computer science, and I was interested in this design stuff, but I didn't have any of it in me. It was Muriel who told me to go to art school. She knew what I was looking for, which was classic design training.

LISA STRAUSFELD: Muriel just had this incredible freedom. She didn't assume the page, in the same way

John Maeda, *Morisawa 10*, 1996.

David Small, *Talmud*, 1993.

she didn't assume the computer screen. She was deliberately very agnostic about technology even though she was at MIT and the Media Lab. She just wanted the content to be whatever it needed to be.

SMALL: The VLW had been in an old industrial building on the edge of campus where they were doing a lot of work with printing. The printing press did not make the leap into the new building, but suddenly they had a lot more computer equipment. There wasn't a graphic design department anywhere else that had a million-dollar computer budget.

STRAUSFELD: We were all expected to have computing skills. For students who were less able to code or were a little rusty, it wasn't ideal. You had to have that facility under your belt to really make it worthwhile, because there was no discussion of programming. It was just a means to another end.

SMALL: We were very interested in what the computer could do to create stuff that no one had seen before. Different kinds of transparency and bringing things in and out of focus. If you looked at what we were doing and compared it to what real graphic designers were producing at the time, it was terrible. The tools weren't good, and we weren't necessarily good designers. We just kept saying, "Computers are the future of design." People didn't necessarily think we were crazy—a lot of people did realize that it was going to be true—but they still looked at what we were doing and were like, "I don't know what you're doing, but it's not graphic design."

MAEDA: In the 1990s, when I was writing computer code to draw things, it wasn't a normal thing to do. A lot of people had these visual art ideas, but they couldn't write software to do it. Steve Jobs had just released his NeXT computer, and I went out and bought one. I opened it up, started running code, and suddenly I was making stuff that no one had seen before. I was making things that changed or were ultra-complex. I was combining a deep understanding of computer science with what I had learned from my classical design training. Not a lot of people had traveled that route, visually speaking. I was drawing millions of lines, and people would look at what I made and say, "How did you make that?"

———————

Golan Levin
Artist | early student at the ACG | professor of
electronic art at Carnegie Mellon University
—

Elise Co
Interaction designer | former student at the ACG |
founder of the design consultancy Aeolab
—

Casey Reas
Artist | former student at the ACG | cofounder of
Processing | professor of art at UCLA
—

Ben Fry
Information designer | early student at the ACG |
cofounder of Processing | principal at Fathom
Information Design

In 1994, Cooper unexpectedly died from a heart
attack. Maeda, who had left MIT to study graphic
design at the University of Tsukuba in Japan,
returned to MIT in 1996 to start the Aesthetics +
Computation Group (ACG) at the Media Lab. The
ACG was meant to continue Cooper's mission of
exploring the intersection of design, art, and technology. But where Cooper's research pushed the
boundaries of graphics and information design,
Maeda was interested in learning how code could
be used to create new, unseen forms.

   During this time, Maeda developed Design by
Numbers, an interactive tool kit that simplified
computational design for non-coders. His goal was
to democratize programming by teaching designers
simple commands that could produce dynamic
images in a one-hundred-by-one-hundred-pixel box
on the screen. Compared to the technical tools his
students were using at the ACG, Design by Numbers

Golan Levin, *Floo*, 1999.

was simplistic, but it set the stage for Casey Reas and Ben Fry to create Processing, a more powerful tool that artists and designers still use today to create interactive work.

MAEDA: Muriel Cooper had died, and there was a search for faculty—someone to carry on her mission. At the ACG we took up all her assets. All the space became our space. It was an exciting time because it was the last time that academia had the edge on computing. We had the most advanced computers on the planet, and I got to recruit people who were the best in the world at knowing what to do with these things. People like Ben Fry, Casey Reas, and Golan Levin.

GOLAN LEVIN: One thing that was really interesting about John's group at MIT was that it was called the Aesthetics + Computation Group. It wasn't called the design and computation group or the art and computation group. There was a certain agnosticism about whether we were artists or designers. We were form makers, we were form seekers.

We were heavily inspired by the kinds of experiments made in the Bauhaus. We were trying to understand the fundamental principles of computational visual form. It meant you could have someone like Peter Cho, who was working on typography, and someone like Ben Fry, who was working on information visualization, and someone like Elise Co, who was working on wearable electronics.

ELISE CO: Something we'd always discussed among ourselves, and something John would talk about, was the idea that we were designers who could use computation and code directly to make the things we wanted to design, rather than using Photoshop. It was about computation as a material rather than a tool.

CASEY REAS: At the time, the barrier to learning how to code was extremely high. I don't think it was on the radar for most designers.

MAEDA: I wanted to broaden who could code, so I created this language called Design by Numbers. I intended to make programming easier for people who are what I call "mathematically challenged."

LEVIN: It was essentially this reduced world of one hundred by one hundred pixels and one hundred levels of grayscale. It was more a pedagogical tool than a tool for doing anything "useful." When Ben completed his master's degree, he and Casey began to think about what it would be like if DBN was more than just an educational exercise. People wanted things like color and more pixels, and that was a reasonable request for design students who wanted to do more interesting things than what they could do in a one-hundred-by-one-hundred-pixel, grayscale world. That was the birth of Processing.

MAEDA: I remember when DBN came out, Ben and Casey built the second version of it. They said, "We need something more powerful." And I was like, "What? This isn't good enough?" I remember thinking, "Maybe you should work on your thesis." I'm so glad that I was wrong.

BEN FRY: Later in the course of DBN, we were seeing how people would stretch it in different ways and try to build ridiculous things with this incredibly limited environment. As the maintainers of the software, we did a lot of toying with how we would approach it differently, or how we would use some of the nice things we liked about DBN and then expand it and get it closer to our own process for creating work.

REAS: For me, the idea of traditional foundational studies was important to Processing. I thought it was another Bauhaus moment. I thought, in the same way that during the Bauhaus era we moved from arts-and-crafts production into industrialized production, it was time to move from industrial production into computer software, information-based production.

I also wanted to change how software was integrated into arts and design education. I thought that the way schools were teaching students how to use

Casey Reas, *RGB-056-006-080-823-715*, 2015.

Photoshop and Illustrator was entirely surface and didn't even begin to explore the possibilities of new media. I wanted there to be a deeper understanding of the medium, rather than just using it as a tool.

FRY: A lot of people would say that having to write the code to produce the page and images was actually a huge step backward from having a tool to do it. But one of the ways John put it that always struck me was this idea that you wouldn't have a painter who doesn't know how to mix paint or work within their medium.

In part, it was a response to tools like Photoshop and Illustrator that allow you to build things, but they separate you from the medium in a way that's not always helpful. More importantly, you're restricted by what the companies building those tools are making available to you. That's a significant problem in terms of your creative output being controlled by a company whose priorities might not be aligned with yours and your best, most interesting, and most challenging work.

———————

Lauren McCarthy
Artist | former student at MIT | founder of p5.js |
assistant professor at UCLA
—

Zach Lieberman
Artist | former student at Parsons School of Design
under Golan Levin | founder of the School for Poetic
Computation

Throughout the early 2000s, Processing started
to spread as professors used the tool kit to teach
a new generation of artists and designers how to
code. While Processing became a foundational tool
for creating expressive code, other tool kits began
emerging, to account for different programming
languages and artistic needs. Zach Lieberman,
a student of Levin's at Parsons and cofounder of the
School for Poetic Computation, developed open-
Frameworks, a tool based on C++. Then in 2013, new
media artist Lauren McCarthy created p5.js, a web-
friendly continuation of Processing that runs on
JavaScript. These materials have pushed the creative
boundaries of what is made with code, and at the
same time they've expanded the notion of who can
create with code.

LAUREN MCCARTHY: Back in 2012, I heard this
lecture by Zach Lieberman at Eyeo Festival. He was
saying, "I know open-source is mostly men right now,
but if you're a woman, you're welcome, too." It was
the first time that I was like, "Oh, I'd like to sit at the
table." It hadn't crossed my mind before.

LEVIN: The environments were put out there by
Casey and Ben and Zach in order to democratize the
creation of interactive graphical environments. It was

91

an open invitation for anyone to make stuff with these tools, but there wasn't an open enough invitation for anyone to contribute to the environment, to the tools.

ZACH LIEBERMAN: It's still a problem, in that these tools tend to be made by a lot of white dudes. I think it's important to have a more inclusive and better community. These tools are trying to make it easy for people to get started and make things. We want more voices and more people at the table.

> "
> I don't know what you're doing, but it's not graphic design.
> "

LEVIN: The important thing Lauren did, in addition to creating a JavaScript flavor of Processing, is that she was also keenly attuned to what one could call inadvertent omissions of approach in the open-source communities behind openFrameworks and Processing. The ways in which these communities did not adequately address issues of diversity and inclusion.

MCCARTHY: p5.js is a reinterpretation of Processing. It takes the initial goals of Processing and asks: What does that mean for today? It means using HTML, JavaScript, CSS, APIS, and mobile webcams—that kind of stuff. But also, in 2013, when we were thinking about it, I was hearing all these conversations about how we can incorporate more diversity into the projects. Instead of trying to retrofit ideas into a project, we wondered: Can we try to build values of diversity and inclusion into the code from the get-go? We were making decisions in every moment, asking: Who are we privileging here? Who are we excluding? Who are we including? How do we make our message more explicit?

LIEBERMAN: Today we have better tools and better communities. It's broadened in some ways. If you wanted to do this stuff twenty years ago, you needed to be at the MIT Media Lab or someplace in academia, and now it's really different. At one point this stuff was new. It's not new anymore. And I think that's exciting. When the technology is new, a lot of what you're doing is very formal; it's about figuring it out. But as the medium establishes itself, then it's more like artistic expression. What does code mean, and how can we use it to tell meaningful stories? Now that we know what the medium is, we can use it in a more expressive way.

◉

PART II : QUESTIONS

INTRODUCTION

ye on Design's greatest and most regular prompt for growth and change is an annual brainstorm meeting that we hold every January. We start with a Google Doc full of questions that helps us focus our harried brains on what we want to accomplish in the coming year. What are we proud of from last year? What could we do better? What are the big stories we want to tell in the year ahead? Every January, we start with good intentions, but inevitably they fall by the wayside as we go about the job of doing our jobs. Still, the questions have done *their* job of lodging in our brains as calls for progress and change.

That's what questions do best. Historically, asking questions and probing a field has never been the most popular pastime. (Just ask that gadfly Socrates.) But it's what leads to answers, and more importantly, action. And, with hope, a field that is more ethical, equitable, generous, kind, thoughtful, and remarkable than we ever thought possible, no matter how much we already believe in the power of design.

Once you open your mind to one or two questions, more tend to follow. In this section, we investigate both the micro (Can a fish be a brand?) and the macro (Can we teach graphic design history without the cult of hero worship?). And of course, plenty more questions linger somewhere in between.

Questions inform the future. But they also present a welcome conundrum: if you ask the right ones, they often result in more questions than answers.

Graphic Designers Have Always Loved Minimalism— But at What Cost?

by Jarrett Fuller

ORIGINALLY PUBLISHED APRIL 1, 2021

When I was a student studying design, the phrase "Less is more" felt like a mantra my professors recited to us in each critique: simplicity, white space, fewer fonts. Along with many of my classmates, I internalized this and produced work that in numerous ways echoed the mid-century designers we were learning about. And for most of my design career, I believed it.

I began to question this dogma after seeing countless corporate rebrands that repeatedly stripped their identities of personality in favor of flat, solid-colored, Humanist sans-serif typefaces. Is less always more? When is less just...less? Thus began a historical quest through the history of design and graphic designers' obsession with minimalism. What started as a particular way of working was flattened to a style—the dominant style we're still living with today.

Since we published the essay, there have been moments when it seems the pendulum would swing away from minimalism, but it always, inevitably, swings back. Whether it's logos or interfaces, minimalism, it seems, will always be canonical. Everything else is just heresy.

————————

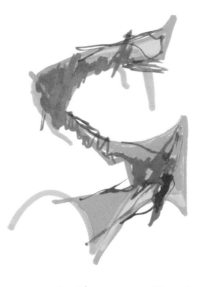

top me if you've heard this one before: Company X announces a new logo with a buzzword-filled press release. "We've been hard at work for months in rethinking how to best represent ourselves to our customers," it reads. "We think this new logo reflects our values by signaling simplicity and approachability." Can you picture it? It's a sans-serif wordmark (bonus points if it's a geometric typeface like Avenir or Proxima Nova, maybe even Helvetica) and set in a solid color (maybe primary, but ideally a tertiary; think a cool greenish blue or warm mauvey red).

What seemed like a fun joke a few years ago quickly moved from trend to meme to the dominant visual style in branding. In the last few years, it seems every big company, from Warner Bros. to Petco to Mastercard to Sam's Club has jumped on the bandwagon, stripping their brand down to basic parts cohering around a homogenized, minimal aesthetic that can sell anything from dog food to data, credit cards to car rides. (There are, of course, brands that divert from this stylistically, but the component parts are the same: flat colors, clean type, and lots of white space—using a serif typeface is hardly a differentiator.) In an article for *Vox* in 2017, the writer Eliza Brooke called this aesthetic "start-up minimalism," following a string of Silicon Valley rebrands including Facebook, Google, Pandora, Pinterest, Spotify, and Uber, who all implemented new geometric sans-serif wordmarks, effectively removing the personality of their previous identities. Brooke wrote that these new, minimalist logos reflect the products they're selling, a visual indication of "how that product will be purchased and delivered to the shopper: digitally, easily, inexpensively, and with a smile."[1]

Minimalism in graphic design can mean all sorts of things in all sorts of contexts, but no matter what, it is clearly popular. A search for "minimalist graphic design" on any visual search engine will return an endless stream of movie posters simplified to icons, band posters reimagined as if they were designed by a Swiss Modernist, Brutalist websites with default black-and-white styling, interface mock-ups stripped of context or detail, and logos upon logos boiled down to basic elements. *Medium*, which got its own version of a minimalist rebrand, is filled with think pieces about creating minimal designs and simple user interactions. Interface design, too—whether a shopping experience, a mobile app, or a social media interaction—is focused on erasing all moments of friction by simplifying the number of clicks, the range of interactions, the paths the user can take through a predetermined flow.

One of industrial designer Dieter Rams's famous maxims, printed on posters in design studios around the world, is "Good design is as little design as possible," and Apple's Jony Ive echoed this when, referring to a new iPhone, he said, "You should almost get the sense that it wasn't designed at all." In the early 2010s, Microsoft, Google, and Apple quickly abandoned 3D, skeuomorphic interfaces (drop shadows, faux leather, paper textures) in favor of flat design, signaling a return to the Bauhausian principles that materials should reflect their use, and decorative flourishes impede function.

1 Eliza Brooke, "Why Does Every Lifestyle Startup Look the Same?," *Vox*, July 27, 2017, https://www.vox.com/2017/7/27/16029512/sans-serif-lifestyle-font.

99

The history of design is a pendulum, and each new aesthetic and approach is a reaction to what came before it. The "new wave" Postmodernists of the 1980s and 1990s were responding to the strict design systems of the Modernists; the bubbly aesthetics of Web 2.0 brands and skeuomorphic interfaces were a visual explosion after years of websites designed by engineers. Yet these movements are largely seen today as outliers—experimental diversions, moments of unnecessary indulgence on the designer's ultimate quest for simplification. For much of the Western world, the design history pendulum always, inevitably, swings back to minimalism. What if this recent spate of rebrands, then, is less a passing fad—a lack of creativity among contemporary graphic designers—and more a natural end point in a profession forever obsessed with simplifying?

The idea that everything could, and should, be made simpler is core to the history of graphic design. The field grew alongside the Industrial Revolution. At the beginning of the twentieth century, as mass production simplified manufacturing processes, moving from the hand to the machine, so, too, did the work of the designer, moving away from ornate decoration to streamlined "modern" images meant to usher in the technological future. In 1910, the architect and essayist Adolf Loos wrote his famous treatise "Ornament and Crime," which decried the excessive ornamentation he saw in Art Nouveau and foreshadowed the upcoming Modernist movement. He called ornamentation primitive and wrote that decoration was for "degenerates." His entire essay, based on racist cultural superiority, repeatedly used words like "criminal," "amoral," and "barbarian" to describe ornament, comparing the arts and crafts from Indigenous populations to that of children.

He called for society to move beyond these old ways into modernity: "The evolution of culture is synonymous with the removal of ornament."[2] The Bauhaus, founded in Germany a decade later and often cited as Modernism's first chapter, saw the political implications of mass production and sought to unify the streamlined manufacturing processes with a matching visual aesthetic. It was at the Bauhaus where Mies van der Rohe, the school's last director, popularized the phrase "Less is more," which became the mantra of designers everywhere. Rejecting ornamentation as "pretentious," many early Bauhaus teachings focused on the abstract reduction of form and the belief that materials should reflect their use. (Later, the architect Louis Sullivan's maxim "Form follows function" would act as shorthand for Bauhaus orthodoxy.)

We see this echoed in Beatrice Ward's now-seminal 1927 essay "The Crystal Goblet."[3] In an elaborate metaphor comparing typography and printing techniques to wineglasses, Ward, a writer and marketing manager for Monotype, explained that typography is a container for thought, and that the design of this thought should not interfere with the message: "There is nothing simple or dull in achieving the transparent page." Her essay—still taught to first-year students in many design programs around the country—helped shape the myth that design should be neutral, a clear container for holding content.

The International Typographic Style, or Swiss Modernism, ran with this and attempted to create a universal (that is, neutral) design system that could be applied to any project, anywhere. Massimo Vignelli, perhaps the most famous designer of the era, infamously only used five typefaces over his

2 Adolf Loos, "Ornament and Crime" (1910), in *Ornament and Crime: Selected Essays*, trans. Michael Mitchell (Los Angeles: Getty Research Institute, 2002), 17–32.

3 Beatrice Warde, "The Crystal Goblet" (1927), in *The Crystal Goblet: Sixteen Essays on Typography*, ed. William Addison Dwiggins (Boston: Graphic Arts, 1956), 13–21.

entire career, applying a similar approach across a range of design projects. Many designers still hold up this era as the epitome of good design, and students are taught—both consciously and unconsciously—to strive for the aesthetics of the Swiss Modernists: embrace white space, use fewer typefaces, align everything to the grid. In short: simplify, simplify, simplify.

Never mind that none of these designers referred to their work as "minimalist." Never mind that the writings of many of those theorists, who were responding to particular demands of a particular era, have become the gospel texts of the graphic designer, and their aesthetic a style to be replicated. "Minimalism" and "modernism" have become largely interchangeable, unable to be pulled apart. I'm guilty of it, too, frequently asking my own students how they could simplify their projects or leave more white space. Sometimes it's easier to teach a set of aesthetic rules.

Yet for the Bauhaus, "Less is more" was not merely an aesthetic position, but also a political one. The promise of the Bauhausian Modernism or the Swiss Modernists was the belief that mass production, intentional use of materials, and functional and modular design were inherently socialist ideals, giving the widest range of people access to the highest quality products. "I think what Massimo saw as the strength of Swiss Modernism was that it was replicable. It wasn't predicated on inspiration or individual genius or talent," Pentagram partner Michael Bierut, who worked with Vignelli for ten years, told me. "You could systematize it. I think that's why it caught on in corporate America."

As Swiss Modernism made its way to the United States, it entangled itself with capitalism, evolving

> **"**
> We can think of start-up minimalism as a twenty-first century, digital-first update to corporate modernism.
> **"**

102

into what we now know as "corporate modernism." In the 1950s and 1960s, as the United States emerged from World War II, the country's biggest corporations hired designers like Paul Rand, Saul Bass, and Lester Beall to update their visual identities. Borrowing from the International Typographic Style of the preceding decades, the logos they created sought to eliminate ornamentation in favor of tightly branded identity systems revolving around carefully drawn, simply constructed marks—a style we might today refer to as "minimalist."

This is essentially how brands are still developed today, especially as the world these brands live in becomes increasingly complex, spread across physical spaces and social media profiles, app icons, and YouTube videos. This complexity makes creating a coherent identity all the more important. How does a brand represent itself across a range of media? We can think of start-up minimalism as not a new trend but rather a twenty-first century, digital-first update to corporate modernism.

Today, minimalism has been reduced to a buzzword that describes a lifestyle, a type of decorating, an Instagram aesthetic, or a decluttering movement, but its roots are in art history as a term first used to describe the simple, geometric sculptures of Donald Judd or the paintings of Sol LeWitt in the 1960s, right around the same time corporate modernism was taking over US businesses. In 1980, Buzz Spector, a designer, artist, and professor, curated *Objects and Logotypes: Relationships between Minimal Art and Corporate Design* at Chicago's Renaissance Society, a show that put many of the mid-century corporate identities of companies like CBS, IBM, and Chase Manhattan Bank alongside the work of minimalist artists like Judd, LeWitt, and Dan Flavin.

Exhibition view, *Objects and Logotypes: Relationships between Minimal Art and Corporate Design*, Renaissance Society, Chicago, 1980.

Spector drew formal comparisons between the seemingly unrelated work by presenting a consistent philosophical underpinning around the control of space and presentation.

Noting the similarities between how Donald Judd wrote about his sculptures and how George Nelson wrote about developing the Herman Miller brand system, Spector argued that both the sculptures and the corporate logos were "strong reflections of social values." In an eerily similar context as start-up minimalism, Spector wrote that decreased government oversight over corporate mergers following the war allowed for the formation of the first truly big US companies like CBS, IBM, International Paper Company, and Merrill Lynch (that era's Facebook, Google, and Apple). Both the artist and the graphic designer, Spector wrote, share a "common faith in the efficacy of form as a means of restructuring society through public exposure to works executed within particular systems of use."[4] These "systems of use," Spector noted, can be seen in both the detailed instructions artists supply galleries in displaying their work and the brand guidelines produced by designers outlining how a logo could and could not be used. For the graphic designer, the single iconographic logo was the visual analog for the corporate mergers. They helped the companies grow while presenting themselves in a simple, clean manner. In other words, their logos made them approachable.

But as ideology became dogma, minimalism was flattened to a style, stripping it of its socialist ideals and turning it into something that can be marketed—a signifier of taste. (The clearest example of this might be the publisher Standards Manual, which has largely built its business in recent years through fetishizing the minimalist logos from history by republishing mid-century brand guidelines as glossy coffee-table books.) In 2015, while a graduate student at Maryland Institute College of Art, designer and brand consultant Sally Maier began exploring the various aesthetics of high and low cultures. Her thesis, "Design Dissection," uncovered how ideas around minimalism subtly signal different values. She found that the more minimal an advertisement's design, for example, the more expensive the product it was marketing.

On the flip side, more visual complexity and larger text on an advertisement often meant cost and affordability played a bigger role in a potential buyer's decision. "It's like the hoarder mentality. You sometimes see rich hoarders, but it's usually associated—class wise—with poverty," Maier told me.

4 Buzz Spector, "Objects and Logotypes," Renaissance Society, 1980, https://renaissancesociety.org/publishing/133/objects-and-logotypes/.

"You want to keep everything because you might not be able to afford it. Emptiness, on the other hand, shows that you have the luxury to decide what to fill or not fill your space with." (As Leonardo da Vinci supposedly said: "Simplicity is the ultimate sophistication.") The same, it turns out, is true in graphic design. Maier diagrammed the white space of magazines ranging from high-end fashion magazines to grocery-store tabloids. Cross-referencing this research with readership data, she discovered that magazines with more white space typically had a readership with a higher average income. It's a surprising correlation, but it shouldn't be. White space is, quite literally, expensive—more white space means more pages, and more pages mean more money.

"From the beginning of your design education, you are trained to appreciate minimal design," Maier told me. "It signifies intention. You're trained to see all the decisions that are being made. This is why you see those logo redesigns where they draw those fake grids on top—it's saying, 'Look, I thought about this.'" I see this in my own students every year. At the beginning of class they always want to add more, to fill up every corner of the page or the screen. Minimalism, for them, isn't sophisticated; it's boring. I don't blame them for thinking this. They are surrounded by a flood of images all the time—on Instagram and TikTok, on T-shirts and storefronts—and they see it all as equally interesting. So why do we value white space? Why do we ask our students to only use a few typefaces in a composition? Because that's how we were taught? Because this is what separates the professional from the amateur? Because the theories of designers a half-century ago got lost in translation and reduced to a style?

We must not confuse simplicity with clarity, minimalism with readability, approach with aesthetics. "What if you saw the daily evidence piled up around you that the world operated with thousands of visual codes, but somehow you would not be taken seriously if you used any of them other than the desiccated form that modernism had devolved into?" Lorraine Wild wrote in her brilliant essay "Castles Made of Sand" (1994). "Could you be forgiven, perhaps, for beginning to suspect that what you were being taught was not actually modernism at all, but habit? Or bizarre fraternity rituals?"[5]

In his recent book on the cultural history of minimalism, *The Longing for Less: Living with Minimalism* (2020), Kyle Chayka argues that minimalism always obscures complexity. The minimalist interface you use to order your takeout, for example, sits above a complex network of gig workers that make sure your ramen is still warm when it arrives. The simple presentation hides the complicated system just below the surface, whether that is the infrastructure for data collection or the multi-conglomerate corporation. (The digital design version of this is the hamburger menu: it gives you a clean layout before revealing an anxiety-inducing number of buttons hidden behind it.) The company wants to appear friendly so it can take your data; the magazine with lots of white space is accessible only to a wealthier readership; the invisible interface is filled with dark patterns to get you to buy, share, browse, or search more.

"Design is all about desire, but strangely this desire seems almost subject-less today, or at least lack-less," wrote the art critic Hal Foster in his essay "Design and Crime" (2002), a loose reinterpretation of Loos's essay. "That is, design seems to advance

5 Lorraine Wild, "Castles Made of Sand," in *Emigre: Graphic Design into the Digital Realm*, ed. Rudy VanderLans and Zuzana Licko (New York: Van Nostrand Reinhold, 1994), 111.

6 Hal Foster, "Design and Crime," in *Design and Crime (and Other Diatribes)* (London: Verso, 2002), 25.

a new kind of narcissism, one that is all image and no interiority—an apotheosis of the subject that is also its potential disappearance."[6] This is the limit of the Modernist project and the blind spots of its creators. The very promise of Modernism—its modularity and replicability—is what made it a convenient tool for capitalism, turning it into a style that helped usher in our current aesthetic blandness. In trying to be everything, it becomes nothing. Call it modernism, flat design, or minimalism, but in the end, the variations on this style have evolved to primarily communicate an aesthetic, or a false idea of taste. Today, the message is the design itself.

This erases the vernacular of local cultures and the plurality of human experience—race, gender, class—reinforcing the myth that design decisions are neutral while creating aesthetic hierarchies of good and bad design. What started as a utopian ideal leading us into an egalitarian future inevitably would become another system of oppression, pushing the tastes of the few onto the many. It should be no surprise that most of the names mentioned here were white and male. (And what of Adolf Loos? He was tried for pedophilia, so maybe he's not the guy whose racist tastes we should be perpetuating.)

To resist these narratives takes more than new maximalist logos, but that'd be a start. "If graphic design reflects the society we live in, it also plays a role in reflecting, perpetuating, and maintaining the social and cultural structures in which we operate," wrote Jen Wang in a 2018 essay called "Now You See It: Helvetica, Modernism and the Status Quo of Design." "We need to challenge the foundation of design practice, to contextualize the history and social role of design as a buttress to imperialism, and to create space in design education for broader

explorations of design aesthetic."[7] In a moment
when we are rethinking how we talk about design
history, decolonizing the industry, and rethinking
design's relationship to power, perhaps this is also
a chance to rethink the cultural signifiers we give
to what we call "good design," or why we value white
space, or why we still think that less is always more.
This could be the beginning of the pendulum swing-
ing back. Until then, to crib the architect Robert
Venturi: Less is a bore.

7 Jen Wang, "Now
You See It: Helvetica,
Modernism and the
Status Quo of Design,"
Medium, December 8,
2016, https://medium.
com/@earth.terminal/
now-you-see-it-
110b77fd13db.

Graphic Design's Obsession with Minimalism

JARRETT FULLER

Brutalist Websites (below)
Although the term proved to be more elastic, the original definition of "Brutalist web design" were sites that lean on default settings: minimal styling, lots of black and white, and little interactivity.

Swissted (opposite)
A poster project from designer Mike Joyce, who reimagines vintage punk, hard core, new wave, and indie rock flyers as International Typographic Style posters.

Nelson Heinemann

ISSN 2631-398X MIDDLEPLANE

American Millennial

Take a Walk on the Wild Side

Utrecht

CHIANGUS

Yves Tumor — Safe In The Hands of Love

zavidova

HOW CHILD

Ashley Cook

Vi Novell 2018 — Caller Maaroig

Studium Generale Rietveld Academi

RAVECONS

LIVE FROM EARTH SHOP

DAPP BOI

Arrangement Studio

Today's Design Is Shaped by Likes. Is That a Problem?

by Sahadeva Hammari

ORIGINALLY PUBLISHED JUNE 22, 2022

n a recent afternoon I visited Dribbble, a popular community and portfolio website used by designers to share and discuss their work. On Dribbble, you can skim through designs for sophisticated banking apps, marketing websites for yet-to-ship start-ups, and designs for crypto mobile apps to buy and sell NFTs. Browsing the portfolios on Dribbble offers an anthropological view of the experience of many designers today. Surveying this work reveals not only the popular style of the moment, but also a flywheel of psychological mechanisms that, for many designers, has taken the rich and complex practice of design and flattened it to a performative, stylistic practice, ultimately both changing what it feels like to be a designer and reducing designers' impact on the world.

One of the most salient characteristics of the work on Dribbble and Behance, and in the world of start-ups more generally, is the eerie similarity of the design work from one designer to the next. The primary technique used by designers in these spaces is to simply remix the dominant patterns and trends created by popular tech companies, ensuring that their work appears as stylistically sophisticated and elegant as the work they're emulating, regardless of what kind of product they're designing or for whom. A podcast app and a banking app and a meditation app seem one and the same, similar styles and elements creating just a few generic interfaces.

Designers who successfully emulate popular design work receive the kind of positive affirmation so many of us have come to crave on the web through our exposure to social media: likes, views, retweets, comments, and other digital affirmations. It's the design equivalent of staging a glamorous-looking photo in a fake private jet and posting it on Instagram.

I call this performative design. Performative design ultimately reduces the practice of design from a wide range of creative, psychological, communication, and problem-solving skills to a narrow practice focused on the reproduction of popular styles and interfaces for the sake of feeling like, and being perceived as, a skilled designer. The success of performative design is measured not by its usefulness or utility in the world—a more traditional method for evaluating the quality of a design—or the meaning the work brings to its users' lives, but rather by how closely the work mimics what is considered "good design." According to this new measure of success, instead of creating a product "as trusted as Airbnb" or "as educational as Duolingo," a design is successful when it "looks like something Apple would make." It is, after all, much easier to mimic successful work than it is to create something new.

The flywheel that motivates performative design can be seen clearly when we look at both a designer's work and the emotional experience behind it. The flywheel starts when designers create work and share it online in order to quench their craving to be seen and applauded as skilled designers. This is the same kind of craving that is woven into so many of our online experiences today, and is also inherent in the fact that, in the internet age, our work as designers is now seen and evaluated on the web.

Second, by reducing "good design" to a narrow collection of styles and interface trends—think Swiss grids, lots of white space,* airy illustrations, and polished icons—designers can more easily replicate "good design" and, as a result, more easily create an image of themselves online that represents what they believe a talented designer's work looks like. Third, designers who participate in performative design avoid criticism in order to maintain the shared belief that the stylistic trends they follow are the definition of "good design." The trap inherent in this flywheel is convincing designers that they're seeing themselves as skilled, successful designers when they replicate the most popular trends of the day, when in reality these designers are simply being applauded for performing like the designers whose work they are emulating.

When I founded my last start-up, the success I pictured for myself was tied more to the image of me walking out onstage at a conference to raucous applause than it was about designing something truly useful or impactful. I didn't do a single user testing session before launching that start-up, for example, because in reality I wasn't focused on creating something useful. Not coincidentally, my designs mimicked the work that was considered "good design" at the time. I wanted to believe that if I created work that looked like "good design," I would inherit the exceptional qualities of the designers I was emulating. It's clear to me now that I was mostly motivated to duplicate others' work because of fear of failure and the desire to be accepted. This is an uncomfortable thing for me to admit. I believed, as Anna Wiener put in her memoir, *Uncanny Valley* (2020), that it was "safer, then, to join a group that told itself, and the world, that it was

Why do designers love minimalism so much? Find out on page 96.

> **It is much easier to mimic successful work than it is to create something new.**

8 Anna Wiener, *Uncanny Valley: A Memoir* (New York: FSG/MCD, 2020), 260.

superior: a hedge against uncertainty, isolation, insecurity."[8]

Designers may create duplicative, performative work for economic reasons, of course. Creating a designer persona online can be an effective and sometimes necessary way to get work and survive in an age of economic turmoil. Performative design's systemic impact, though, is primarily reducing designers' ability to have meaningful positive impact through their work and diminishing the emotional and social experience possible in other forms of design.

The popularity of sites like Dribbble, Behance, and others—and the uniformity of design in so many start-ups—is evidence that performative design has a significant influence on the culture of design and the experience of being a designer. I couldn't find a single comment on Dribbble, for example, that amounted to anything other than a proverbial thumbs-up. How is it that there are so many comments in a creative community and none have even the slightest edge of criticism, constructive or otherwise? The elimination of critique, I believe, stems from designers' fear that their identity as a "good designer" is at risk when critique is present. Joining a community that has implicitly agreed to eliminate critique provides a safe haven for performative design and, in turn, accelerates the adoption of it.

To be a designer practicing performative design, then, is to focus more on developing the persona and visual output of a skilled designer than on creating products or services that have a positive impact on their customers or the designer themself. This approach to design has consequences beyond the individual designer and even the design community—it impacts the broader culture we live in. "When we think of 'good design' or 'good products,'" write Courtney Heldreth and Tabitha Yong in their essay "Racial Equity in Everyday Products" (2021), "we often simply replicate the tastes of those we consider 'experts' in the industry (which are canonically Western-centric and homogenous), and the cultural inputs we've been given. Design especially has dealt with issues of creative savior complex rather than actually aligning our talents with vulnerable communities' needs and increasing their power."[9] In other words, creating work that perpetuates dominant trends in order to receive positive affirmation from like-minded designers, regardless of any real-world impact, can ultimately have a negative impact on culture and society.

Two recently developed financial tools offer a clear contrast between performative and non-performative design. The Robinhood trading app, on one hand, is a perfect example of performative design's success when measured by its execution of "good design." As the folks at Robinhood claim, their goal was to create "a product so simple and elegant that it would revolutionize an entire industry." The designers at Robinhood have indeed created a product that includes all the hallmarks of "good design," including beautiful illustrations and a quirky onboarding flow, but, crucially, they've done little to understand the psychology of people who are trying to manage and invest their money in uncertain times.

To the contrary, as noted in the *New York Times*, "at least part of Robinhood's success appears to have been built on a Silicon Valley playbook of behavioral nudges and push notifications, which has drawn inexperienced investors into the riskiest trading." It's clear that the design team at Robinhood wasn't

9 Courtney Heldreth and Tabitha Yong, "Racial Equity in Everyday Products," Google Design, May 13, 2021, https://design.google/library/racial-equity-everyday-products/.

10 Don Norman, *The Design of Everyday Things* (1988; New York: Basic Books, 2013), 7.

"

Creating a designer persona online can be an effective way to survive in an age of economic turmoil.

"

focused on the nonprofessional investors who were of course surprised by their trading losses, or the people who have become addicted to trading crypto-currencies on their app. They were instead interested in using "good design" to get them to buy risky stocks more often.

The Consumer Financial Protection Bureau, on the other hand, set out to understand the psychology of potential home buyers and designed a three-page "Know Before You Owe" form to help them understand the financial risks of buying a home, easily compare competing mortgage products, and avoid falling prey to predatory mortgage prod-ucts. The simple black-and-white paper document didn't include a single elegant illustration and looks incredibly boring, yet it succeeded in helping many consumers understand the total cost and risks associ-ated with a mortgage and significantly reduced the number of people losing their houses to risky mort-gages in the United States.

Designers on Dribbble and in the start-up world, unfortunately, only see one of these as a success. This echoes a lesson Don Norman articulated in his classic book *The Design of Everyday Things* (1988). Early in his career, Norman was asked to help find the root cause of the meltdown of the nuclear power plant at Three Mile Island. Norman concluded that the design of the power plant's control room was at fault because, although it appeared functional, or even elegant, it was simply too complex for its opera-tors to use safely. "The moral was simple: we were designing things for people, so we needed to under-stand both technology and people," Norman wrote. "Today, I realize that design presents a fascinating interplay of technology and psychology, that the designers must understand both."[10]

For the designers at Robinhood and the Consumer Financial Protection Bureau, it must have also felt different to design their respective products. Designing an app that risks the financial and psychological well-being of its customers in order to create something that designers can call "simple and elegant" is a very different experience of design than working to understand the psychology involved in home buying and improve people's ability to avoid life-altering financial losses. A career spent pursuing these various kinds of success shapes not only a designer's approach to design, but also what it feels like to be a designer.

So what does it mean when the practice of design has become intertwined with the most self-centered and harmful dynamics of the social web? For many, it means a reluctance to engage in the psychological and emotional aspects of design that are necessary for design to function as a tool for substantive impact. Despite how exciting and affirming it can feel to practice performative design, or how useful it might be in terms of building an audience online, it ultimately renders a designer's work static and inert, unable to reach the people that design can, at its best, engage with deeply. In other words, when design becomes performance, "good design" isn't really design at all.

◉

Can We Teach Graphic Design History without the Cult of Hero Worship?

by Aggie Toppins

ORIGINALLY PUBLISHED MAY 29, 2020

et's engage in a thought experiment. Think about what you know about graphic design history. Then omit all mention of design heroes. Also try for a moment not to think about the objects of design. Consider instead the kinds of social forces that surround design as a practice: labor, technology, or politics, for example.

Now let's get more specific. Visualize, if you can, an agrarian culture being reshaped by industrial labor. Imagine leaving the farm for black-smoke-belching chimneys and the din of machines mixed with the chatter of myriad languages. Think about large groups of people migrating across the globe, displaced, but living in close quarters in crowded cities. Imagine the sublime and unprecedented speed of mass production. And then, in your mind's eye, watch the world go to war—twice.

Cultures clashing. Pistons pumping. Bombs dropping. What might it mean to respond to this as a designer? These are some of the conditions that led to Modernism and its utopian goal of bringing order to chaos.

Admittedly, this thought experiment may be challenging. While we can readily visualize a poster, it is harder to imagine worlds. We're more equipped to think about design history through the seductive work of prominent figures. Many students can name a formal feature of Modernism ("it's simple") or possibly even a designer (Paul Rand) before being

11 Johanna Drucker, "Philip Meggs and Richard Hollis: Models of Graphic Design History," *Design and Culture* 1, no. 1 (March 2009): 51–77.

able to articulate the forces that brought this ethos into being.

Since the 1980s, when graphic design history was still considered in terms of movements, it has been common to teach the subject as a progression of styles, with objects made by heroically talented people. This promotes connoisseurship, but it does not explain the underlying causes of design or how it relates to its audiences. Graphic design emerges from social, technological, economic, and political contexts. It's important for those who study its history to connect design and designers to these contexts first and foremost.

Early design historians sought to promote graphic design as a profession. They wanted to distinguish it from commercial art or the printing industry. To do this, they created legacy histories with a cast of brilliant characters to inspire future generations. In a 2009 article for *Design and Culture*, Johanna Drucker compared Philip B. Meggs's groundbreaking *Meggs' History of Graphic Design* (1983) to Richard Hollis's *Graphic Design: A Concise History* (1994). These two books were instrumental in establishing the graphic design canon and are still widely used in courses in Europe and the United States. Drucker offered a respectful and thorough critique, observing that in Meggs's history, design objects are the result of a designer's special genius rather than cultural influences or economic pressures. In Hollis's model, pioneers still instigate change, but this happens within "social circumstances and cultural functions."[11]

Throughout the 1990s, academic journals like *Design Issues* and *Visible Language* challenged historians to write more critical histories that would acknowledge both the social fabric that envelops design and design's role in economic systems. Newer books like Johanna Drucker and Emily McVarish's *Graphic Design History: A Critical Guide* (2008, 2012) and Meredith Davis's *Graphic Design Theory* (2012) offered fresh interpretations of a familiar narrative. These books start by describing shifting cultures, and from there enter historically significant ideas, objects, and people.

Now that graphic design is a more established field, it's time to do away with legacy histories. As Juliette Cezzar noted in a 2019 op-ed for *Eye on Design*, a number of new biographies are emerging to celebrate the underrepresented.[12] While we may not encourage historical understanding simply by adding more profiles to the canon, we do need to study ways of knowing and making from overlooked communities in the past. Graphic design history tells of a singular, professional, and closed field. But the future is pluralistic, shared, and open.

The graphic design industry shrouds itself in capitalist rhetoric that privileges individual achievement over social phenomena. It follows, then, that graphic design history, which is traditionally a discourse of capitalism, would emphasize individual achievements, too. But nothing about this is natural. It is a historiographical conceit.

History writing has a history of its own. In *Thinking about History* (2017), historian Sarah Maza notes that history evolves to reflect the concerns of the present. She describes history as what the present needs to know about the past: "In archaic and hierarchical societies, the 'useful' past is that of monarchs, military leaders, and great dynasties; in a democracy, citizens want to hear about the history of 'the people.'"[13] In the eighteenth century, the task of the historian was to frame nationalistic

12 Juliette Cezzar, "Let's Teach a History of Ideas, Not the History of Individuals," *Eye on Design*, May 10, 2019, https://eyeondesign.aiga.org/lets-teach-a-history-of-ideas-not-the-history-of-individuals/.

13 Sarah Maza, *Thinking about History* (Chicago: University of Chicago Press, 2017), 6.

narratives, but today's historians understand that their goal is to explain change over time and bring the past to life in the present.

Graphic design, by focusing on its own version of monarchs and dynasties, maintains an outdated approach to history that further entrenches it as a hierarchical society. What present-day designers need to know about the past is not, for example, that Jan Tschichold made trailblazing book covers for Penguin. It's more important to understand that Tschichold was one of many designers who responded to his social milieu by developing systems for standardization. The book covers are not self-evident objects. They exemplify an idea that emerged from a social condition. By reflecting on context first and formal qualities second, students of history might recognize that design is in dialogue with culture. They might even see in the Modernist drive to standardize a parallel with today's UX/UI professions. The past is in the present.

Davis's chapter on Modernism in *Graphic Design Theory* opens with an arresting image of a child— a cotton mill worker photographed by Lewis Hine in 1908. Davis skillfully brings to life a time of grossly exploitative labor, innovative technologies, and intensifying consumerism before she mentions a single object of Modernist design. The past is gone and may be difficult to relate to, but in Davis's text, that child worker announces Modernism by putting a face on a radically transformative era. History needs people, but it doesn't need heroes. Davis's book is an exemplary social history of design. In it, no artifact or practitioner operates outside of the world. The Dada technique of photomontage is grounded in politics. The Modernist dream of universal communication emerges from war-torn

"

History needs people, but it doesn't need heroes.

"

societies. The Postmodern fascination with vernacular graphics is problematized in consideration of design's class privilege. Davis's reader is not asked to admire charming forms, but to recognize the ways design comports with cultural flux, even as it contradicts its own rhetoric.

Davis does not fully omit designers. Designers and design objects are secondary, even tertiary, to ideas that manifest from affective forces. It is true that certain people influenced design a great deal. But in Davis's text, even these pivotal figures result from cultural conditions.

In his essay "Changing Attitudes to Graphic Design History in the Digital Age" (2014), Adrian Shaughnessy observes that emerging designers seem disenchanted with the contemporary field while taking solace in history. He argues that "as the future becomes more and more dominated by digital platforms, strategies and methodologies, the reality for many thousands of graphic designers is that their role is increasingly marginalized." Shaughnessy notes that design is often produced using templates, developed under supervision in collaborative teams, and controlled by strategists. "But to eyes disenchanted with the world of digital creativity," he writes, "graphic design's past is being viewed afresh from the idealistic yearning of a return to the designer as individual creator."[14]

And yet, before the computer, designers relied on analogous trades to realize their plans. They worked with typesetters and printers, for example, to produce a single artifact. Design has always been controlled by outside conditions; labor has always been collaborative. Many prominent designers, even if gifted leaders, were supported by teams who created value for their businesses. Individual

14 Adrian Shaughnessy, "Changing Attitudes to Graphic Design History in the Digital Age," in *Graphic Design: History and Practice*, ed. Antonino Benincasa et al. (Bolzano, Italy: Bozen-Bolzano University Press, 2016), 233–38.

creators are, to no small extent, historical fabrications. Let's suspend the cult of hero worship in order to reflect on this myth.

The nostalgia observed by Shaughnessy should inspire designers to examine their relationship to the past as it is mediated by history. Design heroes are mythical—we imagined them, and we can un-imagine them. As a field, we should stop perpetuating the idea that designers are singular change agents who act on culture from outside of it. Rather, we should make visible the complex social worlds in which designers practice.

People Have the Power

———

Three print collectives from history that prove more is better than one

THE DETROIT PRINTING CO-OP

The Detroit Printing Co-op was a site of production for tens of thousands of leftist books, pamphlets, and posters from 1970 to 1980. There, the acts of writing about and debating politics were folded into the activities of page layout, typesetting, printing, binding, and trimming. The co-op drew a wide range of people from across the city, most of whom were involved in movement politics, and printed some of the most important leftist literature of the 1970s. The people who printed at the co-op were mostly self-taught. None had formal training in "the graphic arts" or considered themselves graphic designers. Participants were, first and foremost, motivated by a desire for political and social change. Yet many of the publications printed at the co-op exude raw enthusiasm for the craft of printing, attention to graphic detail, and playfulness with respect to the tools and materials they were using. Members of the co-op didn't relate to the idea of graphic design or print production as wage labor, or a step in their career development, but as a craft with revolutionary potential.

—Danielle Aubert

A spread from *Incoherence of the Intellectual*, 1969, printed by
Fredy Perlman at the Detroit Printing Co-op.

A poster design from See Red Women's Workshop, 1976

SEE RED WOMEN'S WORKSHOP

The feminist print collective See Red Women's Workshop was ahead of its time in the battle to fight sexism in advertising, marketing, and the media. Forty-five women joined See Red between 1974 and 1990. Together, they produced posters, illustrations, post-cards, and calendars in London's South East End and Camden district, funding the venture from sales and community donations. Working collectively was central to the group's ethos: they shared skills and knowledge, produced work that explored personal experi-ences, and never credited one sole member to a print. This hand-drawn design was made for a 1976 calendar but went on to be sold as a separate poster. "Later, we saw a photo by Syd Shelton taken at the 1977 Lewisham demonstration against the National Front and changed the design to use this image—it seemed the most active and relevant illustration of our ideas," said See Red members. "We wanted to show that women were fully involved in these protests and campaigns."
—Madeleine Morley

THE POSTER WORKSHOP

Between the summer of 1968 and 1971, workers on strike, civil rights groups, and liberation movements could simply walk in and commission a silkscreened poster from a collective known as the Poster Workshop in a small basement at 61 Camden Road in London. The idea was that urgent posters could be designed and printed quickly using that cheap, easy, and fast production method in order to respond to critical political and social matters. This particular design was made to advocate for workers' rights when the trade unions were being curbed; the Poster Workshop worked all night on it, designing, printing, and finally drying hundreds of sheets with hair dryers from the neighboring hair salon. Members posted the final prod-uct across the city early in the morning to inform workers of strike action before the start of the morning shift.
—Madeleine Morley

A poster from the Poster Workshop.

Can Fonts Really Help Those with Dyslexia?

by Madeleine Morley

ORIGINALLY PUBLISHED JUNE 26, 2018

This story began as an investigation into the
dubious promises of "dyslexic-friendly" fonts,
but as I was reporting it, I realized that it was
a story about my experience in my own profession
of writing.

I've been contributing to *Eye on Design* for
more than seven years, and when I first began as
a staff writer fresh out of university in 2015, most of
my stories were about how design is really good at
solving problems. I would interview young designers
about their newest projects, waxing lyrical about
how a typeface, poster series, or flashy website
was going to raise awareness around an important
issue and maybe even combat some of society's
biggest problems. Because that's what design was
invented to do—solve problems—and it's what
we intended to wholeheartedly celebrate at *Eye
on Design*.

Over time, we began to investigate more deeply
the projects we platformed. I became interested in
data, academic reports, and the science of design.
And it was while looking into the science behind
projects conceived for people with learning disabilities like dyslexia that I began to see the real-life
implications of design's collective ego, and what
happens when the design press celebrates a graphic
designer's intention without knowing whether
a project really does what it set out to do.

Ultimately, this is a story about what happens
when typography flies too close to the sun, but it's
also a story of the popular design media.* It comes
from a moment in *Eye on Design*'s history when we
were evolving from a website showcasing designer
portfolios to a space of accessible, long-form design
criticism. Today, the overarching message still feels
relevant, because design media continues to churn

See page 16 to
read "If You Love It,
Let It Go (All Media
Is Design Media)."

out stories with clickbait headlines about how a symbol is going to make the internet more accessible, or how a poster is going to eradicate gender stereotypes, without any proof of concept. For me, the piece feels like a reminder that "design for good" still needs to be put under the microscope.

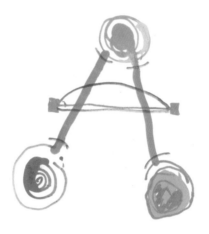

s a child, a cat always became a bat. My name was not Maddy but Mubby. Stranger still, a dog would often take the shape of a bog.

My German mother would sit me at the kitchen table and tell me to read aloud from a German book, and although I was fluent in the language and loved stories, the exercise was painfully boring and difficult. I was frustrated; she was frustrated. One day at school, I was caught reading a book upside down. Finally, at age eight, an empathetic teacher suggested that I might be dyslexic, which a test soon confirmed.

Then began the long, laborious task of memorizing words. While other children seemed to remember the spelling of a word shortly after they'd been taught it, I required far more time-consuming strategies.

A specialist teacher gave me a deck of cards that I went through every day with my parents, and I'd add a new card to it every week. This went on for years. To learn how to spell "said," for example, we wrote the sentence "Silly Alice Is Dead" onto one

134

card and I sketched a gruesome picture of a grave-
stone beneath it. To remember "beauty" and
"beautiful" (the sounding out of "e-a-u" never made
sense to me), I wrote "Big Eyes And Unusual Teeth
+ Y or I F U L" onto another card, and then drew
a picture of a monster. When I spell a word on the
computer today, those sentences sometimes ring
out in my head—as do the pictures I drew to recall
how its letters fit together. I don't rely on them like
I once did, but every so often their singsong rhythms
come back to me like muscle memory.

Today, those struggling with dyslexia will
discover proposed solutions not just from specialist
educators, but from designers who are approaching
the learning disability through type. In both the
design press and major news outlets, I regularly
come across articles lauding a new "dyslexic-
friendly" font, which is always enthusiastically
endorsed by designers. Other projects attempt
to design better reading experiences for dyslexics
through the use of clever plug-ins or colored
backgrounds.

These projects are easy to celebrate, as they
reinforce a popular narrative in the design world:
that design has the power to be transformative and
to make the world a better, more accessible place.
And indeed, for a dyslexic, the promise is an entic-
ing one: Could I have saved all of that time and
energy coming up with strategies and word games
as a kid simply by switching typefaces?

The core idea behind dyslexic-friendly fonts is
that each letter is designed so that it's easier for a
dyslexic individual to distinguish them, thus reducing errors and reading effort. The designers behind
these projects suggest that the bottom-heaviness
of their new typefaces prevents them from turning

upside down for dyslexic readers. Letters with sticks and tails—like *b*, *d*, *p*, and *q*—vary in length so that readers don't confuse them. Many of the fonts' websites, though not all of them, emphasize that these designs are "not a cure for dyslexia" but instead a "reading aid."

While these projects often garner many positive reviews and testimonials, there's little peer-reviewed scientific evidence backing the designs. This is concerning because, just like any other medical or technological advancement, fonts that claim to help a learning disability like dyslexia need to be tested and verified by the scientific community. When a design becomes widely popularized before it's been properly studied—when we pat ourselves on the back before all the evidence is in—it can do more to hurt than to actually aid dyslexic individuals.

To see how valuable these fonts truly are as a reading aid, I reached out to Christian Boer, whose Dyslexie font has been lauded by the BBC, *The Guardian*, *Scientific American*, CBS News, USA Today, and *Dezeen*. It's been highlighted at the Victoria and Albert Museum in London and the Istanbul Design Biennial, and Boer has done Ted Talks about the font and received numerous awards.

Boer's personal story is an all-too-familiar one: when he first began having difficulty learning to read and write, his parents couldn't understand why, especially since his two older siblings had found it so simple. "I saw that everyone at school was faster than me," Boer says. "I thought, 'I'm too tired today,' or 'I'm not in the mood,' or 'I can't focus.' After two years of this, during which the gap between me and the others grew bigger and bigger, I ran out of excuses." Boer was tested by a specialist and diagnosed.

Without a strong support system during his education, Boer developed his own techniques and strategies for coping. As an undergraduate student at the University of the Arts Utrecht, he created Dyslexie—the font he wished he'd had as a child. Boer had always had issues recognizing uppercase, for example, so Dyslexie uses bolded capitals. While traditional fonts mirror the *d* and the *b*, and the *q* and the *p*, Boer's typeface distorts each letter to distinguish them. It slants the extenders and descenders and enlarges the openings to make each letter uniquely stand out. The valleys of *v*, *w*, and *y* are given different heights and levels so that their proportions are obviously different. The *c* is open in a way that makes it distinct from the rounded shape of an *o*.

"After I designed it, I was overwhelmed by how many people reached out to me and wanted to use it, too," says Boer, though he is quick to emphasize that the font is not a cure for dyslexia.

Since Dyslexie has been turned into a business, Boer has received testimonials via email and social media that thank him for his invention. There's also a section on the website entitled "Research" with a couple of PDFs of masters' theses, a bachelor thesis, and a handful of surveys. From this research, the website claims: "About 84.3% of the dyslexics would recommend using Dyslexie font to others." Parents recount stories of how their child nearly dropped out of school but was then reenergized by the font, and even continued on to higher education. There are countless more sincere, genuine reviews: "By the time I got to 'w' I was silently crying," reads one. Another: "Once I saw [the font], I was completely free. It was like a breath of fresh air that had been let loose."

> **"**
>
> **Could I have saved all of that time and energy simply by switching typefaces?**
>
> **"**

137

I don't personally find Dyslexie useful or different, but I also know that what works for some won't necessarily work for others. I do find the testimonials touching. As someone who initially found it impossible to read but now not only finds reading and writing pleasurable but has built a life and career from them, the stories are invigorating.

Dyslexie is similar to other dyslexic-friendly fonts like the open-source OpenDyslexic and Lexie Readable, which also claim to address the problems of mirroring, turning, swapping, and crowding. With these fonts, key differences in characters are emphasized to mitigate confusion. They are predicated on the belief that dyslexia is characterized by letter reversals.

However, decades of scientific research on dyslexia suggests otherwise. When I contacted Dr. Guinevere Eden, a professor in the Department of Pediatrics at Georgetown University and director of its Center for the Study of Learning, she said that reading difficulties actually stem from deficiencies in phonological coding, rather than visual or syntactic sources.

In the late nineteenth century, when doctors first used the term "word blindness" to describe dyslexia, it falsely linked the learning difficulty with the idea of visual distortion—a misconception that persists to this day. But medical research has since proved that dyslexia is not actually a visual impairment. Take the example of a dyslexic child who is shown how to spell "c-a-t" over and over again for hours, then not recognize the word the next time they see it. It's not because they literally can't observe the shape of the letters. It's because they're having problems matching each letter to a sound.

The way our visual system works is that if we see an image in any direction, we still recognize it as the same object. Eden gave the example of a chair: you know it's a chair whether you're standing behind it, in front of it, or to its side. That's why when children learn to read, sometimes they'll reverse letters that look the same. To override this function, they have to use the oral language structures of the brain when looking at words—what we commonly refer to as "sounding out" a word in order to remember it. Typically, once a child has sounded out the word a few times, she moves on to a stage where she begins to recognize the word as an object rather than a series of letters.

A dyslexic child, however, experiences a neurological processing problem that makes it harder to decode a word into separate sounds. Therefore, it's more difficult for them to move to that stage of reading and writing automatically, where a word is recognized by sight. Individual sounds of language become "sticky," and they're not able to be broken apart with ease.

What does all this mean for dyslexic-friendly fonts? Eden says it's unlikely these types of fonts "will help people with dyslexia a great deal. That's because the fundamental problem of dyslexia is mapping the shapes of the letters to the right sound units." The fact that letters are muddled and mirrored is an *effect* of dyslexia; it's not what's *causing* the reading difficulty. Eden says that it's imperative that these new fonts are tested in controlled, randomized studies, and that several of these studies are then published in peer-reviewed journals, before we can say for certain whether switching fonts can actually help dyslexics learn to read. "The motivation behind these fonts is well intentioned.

139

15 Jessica J. Wery and Jennifer A. Diliberto, "The Effect of a Specialized Dyslexia Font, Open-Dyslexic, on Reading Rate and Accuracy," *Annals of Dyslexia* 67, no. 2 (2016): 114–27, https://doi.org/10.1007/s11881-016-0127-1.

16 Sanne M. Kuster, Marjolijn van Weerdenburg, Marjolein Gompel, and Anna M. Bosman, "Dyslexie Font Does Not Benefit Reading in Children with or without Dyslexia," *Annals of Dyslexia* 68, no. 1 (2017): 25–42, https://doi.org/10.1007/s11881-017-0154-6.

But what current research has shown is that there's no relationship between preference and reading rate," she says. "You might like the font better, but that does not mean you are reading faster. It's just an impression. In the end, you have to go with the data."

Most of the projects around dyslexic-friendly fonts have been tested, just not to the degree that Eden suggests. One peer-reviewed study from 2016, for example, explores the effects of OpenDyslexic on reading rate and accuracy.[15] Designed by Abelardo Gonzalez, the font is open source and available as a choice on Wikipedia and Amazon's Kindle. The paper, which compared OpenDyslexic with Arial and Times New Roman, found no improvement in reading rate or accuracy for students with dyslexia, or in readers without dyslexia. A 2017 peer-reviewed report found that Dyslexie did not result in faster reading or accuracy whatsoever.[16] Font preference was compared to reading performance, and the paper concluded that preference is not related to accuracy or reading speed.

"We have to remember that there is such a thing as the placebo effect," says Eden. "Research does suggest that there is a preference for certain fonts, like Arial, where there is less distraction. When my students make slides, I often tell them to use simpler fonts. It's more appealing, a better look—it's a preference." Learning that you or your child has dyslexia can be frustrating. It feels like a setback. It's a realization that you're going to have to put in a lot of extra work and time, which you might not have. "The reality is that children with dyslexia need to be taught how to decode and memorize words, and that happens with hours of work with a professional instructor," says Eden. "That's a lot more effort than simply changing the font on a computer."

One recent peer-reviewed study suggested that the letter spacing of fonts like Dyslexie might affect reading performance.[17] It concludes that Dyslexie is not helpful because of its specially designed letter shapes, but because of its particular spacing settings. Peer-reviewed research has also shown a relationship for all readers between reading speed and the spacing of letters. For dyslexics who have difficulty with "crowding"—how the presence of some objects (for example, letters) interferes with the ability to see aspects of what is being viewed—reading text with greater spacing between letters might be of some help.

Does this mean that designers should go about tweaking letter spacing to create a dyslexic-friendly experience? I asked Eden. "There needs to be more research first," she said. "Repetition and replication is important in research."

Reading the testimonials of multiple dyslexic-friendly fonts, one might wonder, What's the harm in trying them? While more research still needs to be done, at the very least, good can certainly come from the placebo effect. I remember once babysitting a young dyslexic girl when I was a student; she'd been given colorful transparent paper to help her read. (The use of colorful lenses is another disputed technique in research on dyslexia.) She turned to me as we were reading and said she found that with orange, the words felt "less scary." Maybe these fonts, which are so agile and playful to look at, communicate an atmosphere of ease and kindness to a struggling reader, making the activity feel less severe and frightening. The fonts might not be actively helping someone read quicker or with greater ease, but they could help lessen feelings of fear and stress associated with

17 Eva Marinus, Michelle Mostard, Eliane Segers, Teresa M. Schubert, Alison Madelaine, and Kevin Wheldall, "A Special Font for People with Dyslexia: Does It Work and, if So, Why?" *Dyslexia* 22, no. 3 (2016): 233–44, https://doi.org/10.1002/dys.1527.

"

You might like the font better, but that does not mean you are reading faster.

"

the activity. They are a "preference," but a preference with emotional, psychological implications.

We need to see dyslexic-friendly fonts for what they are: a font change that shifts the personality of the letters, but doesn't necessarily affect reading performance. The personal benefits of possible placebo effects need to be weighed against bigger concerns, though. As Eden told me: "The potential of these fonts as highlighted by the press is misleading, and it takes away from the graveness of the situation." The idea that dyslexia might be helped, even minutely, with a quick font change detracts from the severity and seriousness of a diagnosis, and the fact that parents and schools must dedicate extra time and effort for improvement.

This is not to discourage people to continue designing for disability and access. Rather, it's a call for more rigorous testing for these fonts, on par with the peer-review studies that any other research around learning disabilities would go through. Testing pushes research into new corners, sets higher standards, and encourages interest and funding in the field. Otherwise, what are we doing as an industry when we give out awards before having proof of concept? When we write articles because it's a good story, without knowing if the story holds? The process is one that might actually harm those that a design claims to help—ultimately making the world a little *less* accessible.

Can a Fish Be a Brand?

by John Kazior

ORIGINALLY PUBLISHED OCTOBER 6, 2022

At the time of this writing, the entire animal population on the planet has declined by nearly 70 percent since 1970. Warming of one and a half degrees by the end of the century—once an aspirational limit of the global community at the beginning of the twentieth century—has already become a dead-set certainty. To people all around the world, the truth of our climate crisis and the crimes of global capitalism can be seen plainly in the land, in the air, and among the people living in the many communities along the Mississippi River, swimming in the water.

The carp imported from Asia that now dominates the Mississippi and its tributaries has for decades been a raucous representative of ecology as shaped by global capitalism. The branding of an ostensibly unnatural fish in the United States demonstrates two emergent functions that design has come to serve: its capacity to plaster over the already-obscured ecological and societal crimes of the global market, and its application in remapping the now-warped ecosystems of our living planet into yet another revenue stream for the wealthy.

Throughout the twentieth century, design was deployed to prop up false realities about the world around us. While there have never been more modes of distribution for design to confuse the masses, never has design had to work harder to convince people that the heat they're feeling isn't anything to worry about. The "natural" world is disappearing— if it ever was truly natural—and it is the growing project of commercial design and branding to replace the ecological reality of our planet with a more pleasant fare, bearing the label "eco-friendly." Mass extinction notwithstanding.

he Illinois Department of Natural Resources recently asked branding studio Span to rebrand a fish.

The new miracle species that Span concocted (in collaboration with design consultancy Daylight) is called Copi, named for the "copiousness," or abundance, that it promises consumers. Among Copi's other defining traits, according to its marketing team: It is "environmentally friendly," locally sourced, wild, and responsibly caught. Plus, it's fresh and mild-flavored, marrying "well with a range of seasonings." Copi is a "clean, top-feeding" product that is "healthy," high in Omega-3, Omega-6, and protein. Copi is also sustainable, and "significantly reduces carbon emissions from waterways to table."[18]

Copi's sleek new branding could not be more different than its original connotations. The "invasive carp" or the "Asian carp," as it is commonly referred to, is actually multiple species of fish. It's an animal known to "infest" rivers and waterways throughout the Midwest. These fish damage habitats and pose a major threat to the resort and sport fishing industry, thus hurting local economies. It's a "destructive fish," according to the US Fish and Wildlife Service, and a "parasite." No wonder the state wanted to rebrand it.

But is it possible that design can transform a thing so vile as these alien carp into the bountiful, healthy Copi? Can a clean logo plus modernist, low-profile packaging and some studio-photographed shots transform what has historically been an

18 **See** https://choosecopi.com/responsible https://choosecopi.com/fresh-fish.

Span, rebranding of the Asian carp as Copi, 2022.

ecological terror into a local, edible, environmentally friendly animal?

I doubt it. The four species of carp—commonly referred to as bighead, black, grass, and silver carp—are creatures that swim, breathe, eat, reproduce, think, and do all the things living organisms do. They are beings. Copi, on the other hand, is a product—or, more accurately, a pure commodity, illustrated by the fact that Copi in its branded material is represented almost exclusively as an icon of a fish that has no distinguishing features. If there is any part of it that is an animal, it is the fished, caught, killed, butchered, treated, packaged, cooked, and sold parts. Only as a dead, marketable product can the fish transform from "destructive" and "invasive" species to "healthy" and "environmentally friendly" product, from "invasive carp" to "Copi." And branding plays a key role in transforming an animal into a product.

There is no question that the fishing industry and the US government have wreaked ecological havoc by bringing carp from across the planet to the waters of the US Midwest, but these carp were not always the villains. Introduced to fish farms in the 1970s, the carp was originally imported to clear the waters for another fish-made-product in the South, catfish. The carp would eat algae, plants, bacteria, and small animals on the surface of the water, which would in turn make the farmed catfish healthier and supposedly better tasting. Eventually, carp escaped the farms due to flooding and swam as far as they could up the Mississippi River, radically reshaping the water as they went. If we are measuring success as a human or industry might, by population and range, the fish became far too successful for the fishing industry's liking. And worst of all,

19 Ashley Wong, "How (and Why) to Kill a Lanternfly," *New York Times*, October 4, 2021, https://www.nytimes.com/interactive/2021/10/04/nyregion/lantern-fly-nyc.html.

it threatened the habitat of many popular sport fish like walleye and crappie. What was known as the Asian carp became infamous for the way it leaps from the water to attack fishers (only one of the species, the silver carp, actually does this) and critically threatened a billion-dollar fishing industry with collapse.

Typically, there are two responses to this sort of insurrection from an invasive animal. The first is to simply try to wipe it out. A recent example of an extermination campaign organized by the US government has been the response to the spotted lanternfly: "Don't hesitate. Kill it," reported the *New York Times*.[19] Several task forces across different states, including the National Aquatic Nuisance Species Task Force and the Asian Carp Regional Coordinating Committee, along with the US Army Corps of Engineers, have organized information and technological weaponry against the fish. The design of information, fliers, and PSAs for invasive species are aesthetically similar to wanted posters. The animals, while not explicitly accused, are in essence presented as lawbreakers and bandits. Even the logo of the Asian Carp Regional Coordinating Committee is of a carp in distress (or dying) as a result of the electric fencing that has been used to control the spread of carp populations.

But if you can't beat 'em, sell 'em. In the now decades-long, state-sponsored campaign against the Asian carp, Copi is interestingly not the first attempt at a rebrand. The fish have also been given the name "silverfin" and "Kentucky tuna" for largely the same reasons the Illinois government has now dubbed it Copi—to make it sound more appealing as something to catch and eat. But approaching Span studio for the rebrand marks the first time a professional design agency has been hired for the task. The idea that these fish might offer something new and good to the world is the best—and maybe only— thing this design endeavor has going for it, even if their eyes are fixed on the economy and not so much on ecology. The "invasive" label the fish has endured for so long is a kind of branding, after all, even if it doesn't come with a squeaky-clean design.

But the Copi rebrand is fundamentally flawed in the same way that bringing the carp species to the United States in the first place was flawed. The marketing scheme obscures the history of how and why carp got here, and it ignores the new eco- logical reality that has resulted. While the wanted posters and kill campaigns wrongly make it appear as if the fish themselves have committed a crime instead of the fishing industry, the media and mate- rial at least are able to indicate to us that a crime has taken place, that something is deeply wrong in these waters.

With the introduction of Copi, the crime has suddenly vanished for those with no knowledge of the fish's history. Once a blunder on the part of the catfish industry, the overabundance of carp is now sustainable. With a new image that can be quickly shared, posted, and distributed through social media, the new Copi marketing campaign has the potential to dominate the common narrative about what these fish actually mean to the rivers and lakes they now occupy. With the history, culture, and ecology cut away from the carp, what's left is the product and the consumer. And like the catfish industry before it, the only thing that matters is the commodity and what- ever it takes to make sure the fish-farming industry keeps its profits growing—doubling down on the logic that led to this crisis in the first place.

The peril of this approach is found in another famous example of a government marketing a particular fish: Norway's Atlantic salmon. Today, you will find salmon on pretty much any sushi menu you come across, in Japan or abroad—but this was not the case before the 1990s. In fact, the salmon that are local to Japan were known to carry unhealthy parasites and had to be cooked to be eaten. But in 1985, the Norwegian government launched Project Japan to market the "surplus" of salmon in Norwegian waters to a nation that loved seafood.

Because of overfishing in local stocks in the Pacific, the country was no longer able to sustain its own fish supply. Switching the local Japanese name of salmon from *sake* to *sāmon*, alongside a targeted marketing campaign, resulted in the value of export doubling by 1991. Within a decade, the fish had become a staple of sushi restaurants around the country. Today, the Atlantic salmon that Norway built its industry around is under threat of extinction—its population has been cut in half since Project Japan was launched. The species has been weakened by the fishing industry and the many diseases and spread of sea lice that emerged from industrialized farming.

In 2021, the artist duo Cooking Sections created an exhibition for Tate Modern, London, focusing on the way that fish farming has changed the Atlantic salmon. Notably, the color salmon itself no longer emerges naturally in the fish farmed for sushi, as the pigment occurs in the fish only given several dietary and environmental factors in the life cycle of a non-farmed salmon. In order to give salmon its famous salmon color, farms have to feed them artificial pigments. Industry standards for salmon color include Pantones 1555U, 1565U, 487U, 1635U,

1575U, 157U, 486U, 1645U, 1665U, 485U, and 2347U. All can be found on the official SalmoFan.

Despite the way that the commodification and industrialization of the Atlantic salmon has driven the species toward extinction and changed the creature on such a fundamental level, the story of Project Salmon is understood as a success. And from a marketing perspective, it is. In much the same way, Copi may end up being a great success story, but that does not mean it will be good for the fish or the ecosystem. Headlines about invasive carp are more concerned with monetary losses in the fishing industry—hardly ever the health of midwestern freshwater ecosystems. And no wonder: the fishing market of the Great Lakes is valued at $7 billion, while the money spent to combat the increasing number of invasive fish species introduced by the fish farming industry along the Mississippi and connecting waterways pales in comparison.

The best evidence that the state and the fishing industry are more interested in saving money than in saving the ecosystem is that they thought branding and marketing could solve the problem at all, versus education or making a structural change to the fish industry itself. It is the natural arch of capitalism to sow ecological crisis—to create scarcity in order to drive up value. With Copi, the US government is trying to brush over an ecological catastrophe that it created in the name of a healthy, profitable catfish market. Suggesting that the only way to live in harmony with a species is to make that species into something to exploit has unfortunately become the norm in capitalist society. Examples abound in whales, tuna, cod—follow pretty much any fish you recognize as sold in markets or

20 John Berger, "Why Look at Animals?," in *About Looking* (New York: Pantheon Books, 1980), 2.

restaurants, and you will find ecological mess in its wake. And in combination with warming waters and global fishing stocks, both freshwater and saltwater have been devastated by rapacious industry.

"To suppose that animals first entered the human imagination as meat or leather or horn is to project a nineteenth-century attitude backwards across the millennia. Animals first entered the imagination as messengers and promises," wrote John Berger in his 1980 essay "Why Look at Animals?"[20] To brand animal species, especially the ones that embody the crises that industry has sowed in our shared habitat, is to project this attitude forward into the future. It is to continue to harbor a delusional belief that capitalism, which has in increasingly rapid succession proven that it can only relate to ecology through exploitation and extinction, has not already brutalized the habitat of our future, but will instead set the ecology of the Mississippi River and Great Lakes to something that could be credibly assessed as balanced, healthy and "copious."

What's the Point of Design Education?

by Rachel Berger

hat is the point of a graphic design education? What should we be teaching students who think they want to be graphic designers? Is it a particular skill set? A mindset? A history or collection of histories? How can design educators rewire their inherited beliefs about how and what to teach?

In October 2022, a global group of design educators convened for a frank and wide-ranging exploration of these and other timely questions. Many students come to design by way of a love of drawing, an interest in popular culture, or a capacity for problem-solving. They seek training that will give them a professional outlet for their creative skills. For Sadie Red Wing, James Chae, and Kaleena Sales, this is just the first layer of what a design education can do. They describe the immense power and responsibility of learning to communicate through visual language—to address climate change and other big systemic challenges, to contribute to knowledge about people and cultures who are under-researched, to breathe new life into endangered languages, to be an emancipatory tool to fight oppression.

———————

Sadie Red Wing
Assistant professor of graphic design and Indigenous
visual culture, OCAD University, Toronto
—

James Chae
Assistant professor of design, Hongik University,
Seoul
—

Kaleena Sales
Associate professor of graphic design and chair
of the Department of Art & Design, Tennessee State
University, Nashville

RACHEL BERGER: When I close my eyes and imagine a California College of the Arts graphic design studio course, it's maybe twelve to fifteen students, mostly women, mostly Asian or Asian American. Maybe two white students. Many of the domestic students are queer. What's your version of that? Who is in a typical classroom in your program?

SADIE RED WING: This is my first time teaching extremely diverse classes. The average class is twenty-five to thirty students. About half are from Canada, mostly from the vicinity of Toronto. At most I have two Black students, four Indigenous students, and four white students in each class. The other half is strongly international: Taiwan, China, Japan, Iran, Iraq, Pakistan. Maybe a quarter are queer. In each class, I've got one or two that have worked professionally and are coming back to school to get the degree or are at the age where they have families and family needs. There are a lot of multiracial students in my courses. They definitely have a lot of vulnerability in asking, "Do I pick a side if I'm three different identities?" I'm also seeing students more openly acknowledging it if they have a learning disorder.

JAMES CHAE: My typical classroom is twenty to twenty-four students, pretty much 100 percent domestic Korean, and about 70 percent female. In terms of LGBTQ identity, it's not as open, although I do occasionally have a couple of students who are out. It's pretty homogeneous. My female students are primarily aged nineteen to twenty-three. The male students have to do about two years of military service, so their age range is nineteen to twenty-seven at the oldest. Korean society is quite patriarchal, so the range of ages plays directly into the gender dynamic, which is something that I always try to address.

KALEENA SALES: Fifteen students, nearly 100 percent of whom are Black. A mix of male and female. A lot of students from large urban cities in and around Tennessee, like Memphis, Atlanta, and Chicago. Not a lot of other visible diversity.

BERGER: What should we be teaching a student who thinks they want to be a graphic designer? Is it a particular skill or set of skills? Is it a mindset? Is it a history or a set of histories?

RED WING: As a graphic designer, you're powerful. You have somebody's language in your hands. Graphic designers are also powerful because we can give visual form to anything. We help think about what the look of everything is going to be. As educators, we're training that next generation to be mindful of that power and not to abuse it in any way.

> "
> As a graphic designer, you're powerful. You have somebody's language in your hands.
> "

156

SALES: I've been reading *Pedagogy of the Oppressed* (1968) by Paulo Freire. He famously described education as an act of love, and he's on my mind in relation to this question. Increasingly, I think of education as an emancipatory act. And language, to Sadie's point, is at the center of that. Teaching students to communicate in not just oral or written language, but visual language, can work as an emancipatory tool to fight against anything that oppresses. It's about teaching them how to own what they care about and what they want to say. Educators show students that the tools are there, and how to recognize ways to solve whatever problems they're hoping to solve.

CHAE: I'd like to build on what Kaleena said about emancipatory acts. One big learning curve I had coming to teach in South Korea was that culturally and educationally, for Korean students, being asked a question is incredibly confrontational. In a US environment, a question is a way of saying, "I want to get to know you and your work." For my Korean students, a question means, "You've done something wrong. Your work has flaws." So I am pushing my students to ask questions of each other and ask questions of themselves, and also to look at questions as a starting point rather than a critique.

Now that I am an educator, I find myself reconsidering some of the things I myself learned. Over the past twenty years, Korean typesetting has basically been taught in a Western way. That is a product of the technological tool being Adobe and the fact that a lot of Korea's educators were educated in Europe and the United States. So we are having to adapt Hangul, a writing system that is drawn in a square grid and has movement both horizontally and vertically, to a horizontal baseline that moves primarily horizontally. I'm trying to rewire some of my own typographic training and view this opportunity for innovation as a gift that we can give our students. But that requires us as educators to acknowledge that gap and educate ourselves to foster that kind of innovation.

BERGER: Kaleena and Sadie, do you have strategies or advice for James about how to disrupt the patterns of our own educational context?

RED WING: I may not have answers, but I definitely agree that there is a great need, particularly in encouraging students who want to work with non-Western languages and/or within their traditional languages. I think some of us have struggled with this because not being fluent in a particular language makes it feel hard to critique, mentor, or encourage students to become better at designing and writing in that language.

There's also a lot of opportunity to revitalize languages that are indigenous to the continent of North America and on the verge of extinction. We have Indigenous communities wanting to work with universities, particularly art and design schools, but there aren't enough educators in this space to do that, handle that, or protocol that. I think part of it is that hesitancy of not being able to translate. It sucks that we can't move past that concept of fluency, and we're dropping opportunities that students are looking for.

SALES: I think a lot of us are on this journey of unlearning and relearning. I can speak to it from the perspective of teaching at an HBCU (historically Black college or university). I have mostly Black students, and my students struggle with typography. In my early years, I was teaching the way I had been taught—International Typographic Style and all that. When my students presented work that was reflective of their culture—my culture—and there were textures and colors and dynamic elements, I tried to rein them in, saying, "No. Try to do it really simple, clean, and streamlined." They struggled with that, and it took me too many years to figure out that I should not be pushing their design aesthetic to fit into this box that it didn't want to be forced into.

Now I encourage them to consider and explore how their environment, culture, and experiences seep into their design aesthetic, and how that comes out in their type choices and design choices. I'm more conscious of the words I'm using when we're doing critiques. If something isn't working, it's because it's not communicating what it needs to. But I'm not going to criticize the design because it doesn't fit into Western standards.

That said, I'm also hyperaware of the legacy of cultural assimilation in this country, particularly for Black people wanting to find success and job security in an industry where they are the minority. As critical as I am of Western design standards, and as much as I want my students to embrace their culture and their identity, I try to refrain from being too personally critical if a student chooses to follow a more main-stream approach in their design. My students want jobs, and I feel like one responsibility that I have as a design educator is to help them find success in this field, according to their needs, not mine.

BERGER: We've talked about what we want for our students, and I'm curious what your students want from you. What are they hoping to get out of their education? And how do you respond or redirect them?

RED WING: Sometimes I've just got to be the cheerleader. I try to boost the confidence of those underrepresented students who probably identify with me the most—any girl who might have lighter brown skin with really dark hair, from South America, the Middle East, or elsewhere around the globe. Sometimes it's all about getting these students to be confident, to be able to explain their process, to be persuasive communicators when they find themselves in an interview or a professional situation.

When you're underrepresented, there aren't enough mouths giving definitions and explaining how a certain aesthetic may be beautiful. A lot of my students want to express Chicana or Chola culture. Sometimes they just need to hear more adjectives explaining that visual culture. It's a demographic that needs designers expressing the beauty of its identity. I try to help my students communicate an underrepresented identity in a professional way that is less like slang or a subculture, and shows that its expression is valid just like any other identity.

SALES: My students want to make a living doing something they enjoy, so they are coming in wanting to know tools and techniques, the how-to for this or that. They like doing fun designs for T-shirts or album covers or flyers or posters. They're not always looking at future trends. They're not necessarily thinking about major issues plaguing the industry. Meanwhile, I'm saying, "Sure, you can learn the tools, but what can you do now that you know the tools?"

Our vantage point in how we're looking at design is a bit different. I'm thinking about how design can be used to address big systemic issues. And my students are like, "Yeah, but how can I make this flyer?" They're not wrong! We're just looking at things differently.

I have to be sure to value what they're seeing as important. I have to value their pursuit to learn tools, not dismiss it. And hopefully I can also open their eyes to the value in using design as a problem-solving tool.

CHAE: The first few years I was teaching in Korea, the students really struggled when I said, "You can do whatever you want!" To give some background, in the culture of critique in Korea, there's this word that I really detest. Students will come and ask, "Can I get a *kompom*?," which is a Koreanized version of "confirm." They're basically asking, "Did I get it right?" It's rooted in what I was talking about earlier, about a question being experienced as criticism.

I think there is a change going on in our critique culture. In the past couple of years, students have stopped using that word as much. Now they come to me and ask, "Can I get some feedback?" I think this newer generation of design students is eager to explore their own topics. Students who come to me are looking for an experience that is a bit more open-ended and free compared to some of the other classes they take. That said, those students are in the minority within my general campus population. A lot of the students are looking for a more directed, tool-based experience. I think the pandemic had a corrosive impact on that expectation. In the distance-learning environment, it was much easier, and in the short term effective, to do tool-based and results-oriented design work. Students who've only been in remote learning situations got too used to this.

SALES: Whenever I've tried a facilitator format, where it's a more student-led, open-ended approach, the students struggle. I think it comes from a distrust of their own instincts and a reliance on an educational

> "Sure, you can learn the tools, but what can you do now that you know the tools?"

system that tells them A + B is C. Do it that way. Don't think outside the box. Do you see that in your programs?

CHAE: You're right. Our undergraduate students are interested in things, but they're not really sure how they want to speak about them. One thing I am learning is that you can still throw the students an open-ended brief, but it's really the class-to-class work that fosters and pushes them, that empowers them and builds that confidence.

RED WING: We're trying to get students to stop relying on Google Images or premade templates so they can create more original work. The challenge that some of them are having is they want to see examples of what they should do, but when we show them examples, they basically submit replicas of what we showed. They're probably assuming that that's what we want to see, but we're just trying to show the depth of the work that goes into creating something original.

BERGER: This is a conversation about the point of a graphic design education, so to close, I'm curious why each of *you* decided to get a graphic design education.

CHAE: I came to graphic design through web design. I had dabbled in high school and paid attention to the link sites that were really popular in the late 1990s and early 2000s. I wasn't the best student, so I was not looking at great prospects if I pursued college purely on my academics. But I had always had an interest in the arts, and I saw an opportunity to go to an art school if I invested time and attention.

Career was one of the motivations of my undergraduate degree. Early on, I really enjoyed the applied

162

arts. I know that's a term that we don't really use anymore, but seeing the commercial application of art skills was powerful for me. There was a practicality to it, too, because I could get a job and establish a career using my artistic skills.

My graduate degree was motivated by a desire to invest in my own personal work and change the path of my career. I had always had a strong artistic spirit in my practice, even as an undergrad, so being able to spend two years focused on myself allowed me to revisit that studio practice, develop that voice, and spend some time finding out what design means for me.

One of my other core ambitions for pursuing a graduate degree was to qualify for faculty positions in South Korea. I grew up in Seoul, and I had always wanted to work in South Korea. I saw the demands of corporate life on my dad, so I knew that that wasn't the route I would take. But I knew that being a professor in Korea is pretty prestigious, and that the working environment is a bit more independent.

SALES: I grew up drawing. All my life I said, "I'll be an artist!" So I was a studio art major in college. Around my junior year I started asking, "What am I gonna do with this?" One day, I was flipping through *Essence*, and I saw "art director" on the list of people who work on the magazine. I started researching what that meant. I like problem-solving, so the intellectual challenge that I thought advertising art direction provided felt like a good fit for me. I went to VCU's Adcenter (now Brandcenter) and pursued a master's in art direction.

I worked as an art director for a couple of years, and I also started teaching as an adjunct graphic design instructor, which I loved. I was told that if

I wanted to keep teaching, I should get an MFA. So I went back and did an MFA through the distance learning program at Savannah College of Art and Design. The VCU program was great at teaching me how to think strategically and conceptually, and SCAD gave me technical skills that I had been missing.

And now I'm back in school, again! For me, pursuing this doctorate is similar to something James said. I'm carving out space to focus on some things I've always been interested in, and forcing myself to make the time to truly understand what research in design means for me. A lot of people use the term "design research" when they're really talking about user testing. My research is about value systems around Black aesthetics, particularly in relation to challenging Eurocentric design "norms." So I'm beginning this work by exploring big broad questions like: What are my research paradigms? What do I believe about how people learn things? Is there one form of reality? Or multiple forms? I'm wading through all of that, and it's really exciting to think it through. Ultimately, I hope to make a small contribution to knowledge about people and cultures who are under-researched.

RED WING: What got me into graphic design was the lack of graphic design expressing any type of Indigenous culture to the United States. Growing up in the late 1990s, particularly coming from a poor community, it was hard for me to find T-shirts or anything that had Native American designs. Fortunately, I was in community with creatives who said, "Instead of going to the mall and getting corny posters at Spencer's, I'm gonna make my own T-shirt designs and album covers and flyers."

I went to the Institute of American Indian Arts in Santa Fe, the only tribal college that has a degree related to graphic design. To get the degree, we had to take a lot of non-design classes. Being in those spaces and being in those critiques, I heard a lot of the terminology I use to this day, like "sovereignty" or "traditional ecological knowledge" or "visual language."

After graduating, I took an internship at NASA. I learned a lot, but it wasn't for me, and I knew I didn't want to go back home to South Dakota. I googled "top master's program graphic design," and North Carolina State University came up. I thought, "Okay, I can go to NC State, pay state tuition, and sneak out to the basketball games over in Chapel Hill." NC State was a culture shock because I had been so immersed in an Indigenous community. At that time, a lot of the research was on future trends, like artificial intelligence and virtual reality. I was thinking, "Hoo, this is really wealthy stuff. This might not work in my reservation." I realized that we have to start developing the framework of what Indigenous design is in the United States and Canada.

Building awareness about the history of Indigenous design here could be particularly helpful for an important new trend: combating climate change. I don't think people can envision what they're striving for because they can't conceive of what the land looked like before colonization destroyed it. The United States has eliminated that visual image for people. I can help paint that picture—how we designed societies to function, how we were able to keep this area sustainable.

Ask the Educators

What is the future of design education? After a decade of publishing interviews with design educators on the *Eye on Design* website, one thing has become clear to us: there's no single, coherent vision, but rather many possible futures for design education.

If design pedagogy in the twentieth century was defined by a drive toward modernist, rationalist purity, many of today's educators are teaching with intersectional politics front of mind. We pulled from our archives conversations with six educators sharing their thoughts on reshaping, and questioning, our industry's past and present. The interviews have been condensed for space.

FOREST YOUNG
MFA senior critic in graphic design, Yale School of Art
https://aigaeod.co/forestyoung
—
You've done a lot of thinking about possible futures for design. What does this mean to you today?

There is an urgent need for guardrails to ensure that future design, or any kind of design pedagogy, isn't framed by a privileged perspective or overly focused on either the historical or the future. Design must defy the constraints of the past while simultaneously not succumbing to a glamorized novelty of something that has yet to be created. Like history, the future is not apolitical. It can be trapped inside of a settler-colonial mindset: it can be a space to plant a flag.

So now, whenever I talk about future design, I refer to it as both an imaginative way to think about what is yet to be and a critical act of looking backward. It is an attempt to shine a light in both directions. This rearview mirror allows us to see who was left out of certain conversations. That was a fundamental shift for me—this imperative for futures to be truly plural. I think that's a new kind of urgency: to see the damage of 2020 as a result of not imagining plural futures, and to realize how much future design had been focusing on a rarefied group of benefactors.

J. DAKOTA BROWN
Designer, writer, researcher, and instructor at School of the Art Institute of Chicago and the University of Illinois at Chicago
https://aigaeod.co/jdakotabrown
—

How do you prepare students to enter a world where they are working under conditions of a climate crisis and reactionary politics?

Design programs radically diverge in what they offer (or even make time for) outside of studio courses. And students are understandably focused on the kind of professional training that will make the immense cost of college worth it. Then, as they enter the field, they face unprecedented expectations of flexibility and versatility. They are coached to ceaselessly adjust and retrain, but they aren't offered a lot of space to question where those compulsions come from or why they exist. The emphasis is always on transforming yourself to meet social demands, which defers the question of transforming society to meet human needs. Academia is definitely not the only way to prepare—in fact, the most important educational spaces for me were always elsewhere: in reading groups or around little magazines.

NONTSIKELELO MUTITI
Director of graduate studies in graphic design, Yale School of Art
https://aigaeod.co/nontsikelelomutiti
—

You work and teach a lot on the edges of typography, redefining what it is and what it could be. Could you talk about that?

The cultures within the space now known as Zimbabwe do not have writing systems that are formally recognized. There were pictograms painted on rock faces or walls and also beaded adornment with codified meaning. I was not taught about any of these ways of articulating myself. Writing and reading has always come with this colonial layer, even when we are reading local languages typeset using roman characters. And so my way of articulating myself has come with this colonial layer of using English, using written form, and reading texts that are set in global characters. When I come into a space of teaching, I'm thinking about typography and letterforms from that position. What are the modules for writing, or for visual meaning-building?

NICOLE KILLIAN
Codirector of the Design, Visual Communications MFA and associate professor in the Department of Graphic Design, Virginia Commonwealth University
https://aigaeod.co/nicolekillian
—

Can you explain what is meant by "queering design education," and how you think educators should be going about it?

When we talk about this idea of queering design education, it's mainly about elevating voices. It's figuring out how to get students to feel like they have more agency in these systems inside of which we all have to maneuver.

Design education has been stale for a really long time. I think educators need to be constantly unlearning what our own educational background was and asking ourselves: What are the actual needs of the bodies in front of us? And not just in a service-provider way. The students in our classrooms want to see people who look like them. They want to see people succeeding who sound like them. So we have to really rethink how we share knowledge. Unlearning or de-skilling is essential, I think, in taking away the hierarchy in the classroom.

These are concepts that are unsettling for some people who have been teaching for a while. Sadly, I think a lot of people in education teach because they like the power they have, and that is scary to me. We need to remove that power and figure out how to create a space where people feel comfortable and excited to be a designer, rather than siloed at their laptops and trying to "win" against their peers.

SAKI MAFUNDIKWA
Founder and director, Zimbabwe Institute of Vigital Arts
https://aigaeod.co/sakimafundikwa
—

There have been conversations lately about authorship in type design—about who's allowed to design typefaces for different scripts, who gets to critique their quality, and what being native to a language, or a region, means. What's your take on these issues?

What I have greater issue with is the buzzword du jour: "decolonization." Here I declare myself the police (along with other Natives). Again, I raise my eyebrows at all this debate and interest among people who have no idea what it means to be colonized. Who feels it knows it—WE the colonized have to lead that debate. Nothing irks me more than "intellectuals" and self-appointed "experts" waxing philosophical about decolonizing design education. My very good friend and partner in crime, Sadie Red Wing, and I ask the very crucial question: What are they decolonizing to? Only someone who has experienced the sting of colonization can decide that question. We are the ones with the Indigenous knowledge systems that become the new curriculum. I'm fond of saying that our future lies in our past, for there lie our greatest achievements and contributions to the development of humanity. We have done the research and have the authority to author new textbooks and course material that our students can relate to and find relevance in. We have to decolonize decolonization.

GAIL ANDERSON
Chair, BFA Advertising and Design
departments, School of Visual Art
https://aigaeod.co/gailanderson
—

Do you have any advice for young designers of color?
   For a designer of color embarking on their first big design job, I'd say: Take a deep breath. Some well-meaning colleagues will say something that will make your head explode, but step back instead and try to turn it into a teaching moment (as corny as that sounds). Make sure to pay it forward and mentor the designers of color you meet as you move up. Teach. Organize. Help.
   I'm always surprised and a little disappointed when people say they don't have time to "hold the door open" for young designers. Not everyone wants to teach—I get it—but there are other opportunities to mentor young designers, like through internships. Overseeing interns can sometimes be like herding cats, and I know that, yes, sometimes it's easier to just do it yourself rather than sit down and explain things to a confused intern, but it's so incredibly rewarding to watch a student or intern blossom. You owe it to your profession if you had a teacher or boss or mentor who helped shape your career, or even your life. It's good karma. Why risk a cartoon anvil falling on your head?

INTRODUCTION

he first known use of the term "graphic design" appeared in a 1917 California School of Arts and Crafts (now CalArts) catalog describing a new class called Graphic Design and Lettering: "Graphic design deals with the principles of lettering and commercial work and the various processes of reproducing the drawings." We've come a long way from thinking of our work simply as reproducing drawings. In the last century, graphic design has evolved to encompass both print and digital elements, systems of distribution, social networks, and even speculative works of art.

Every generation of graphic designers attempts to redefine what graphic design is, the through line being that it always responds to the current moments and contexts. As those in and around the field debate the issues of the day, they begin to redefine design, pushing forward until the next generation picks it up. In this way, design is an inherently future-oriented activity. The act requires both responding to present circumstances and imagining potential futures. Think about branding: in designing a brand for a company, the designer is projecting into the future, imagining how that company could represent itself. In conceptualizing a building or a space, the designer speculates how its inhabitants will one day use it. When that brand and that building are put into the world, those futures are made real: the future becomes the present.

The heated debates between Modernists and Postmodernists and the Twitter arguments about whether designers should learn to code are long gone. The questions of our time involve the climate crisis and hyper-capitalism, labor practices and anti-racism. These live within and around the perennial questions of form and content, style and meaning. In taking stock of what it means to be a designer today, we can point toward more desirable futures.

Conspicuous Consumption

by Cliff Kuang

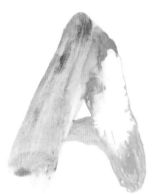 while back, I saw a tweet from the global design consultancy IDEO touting the sustainability work it had been doing for H&M. I'm still a sucker for IDEO stories—the halo effect from the years I spent admiring their work. The project in question was new packaging, which had won awards from D&AD and my old employer, *Fast Company*. On D&AD's site, there was a video of earnest-looking young innovators with Sharpies in hand, surrounded by glass walls adorned in scales of Post-it notes. And what did those teams—"from branding, production, and logistics, all designing shoulder to shoulder"—come up with?[1] A paper shipping envelope, with a blank label that can be printed with the logos of H&M's various brands, such as COS and Weekday. All told, one hundred million had shipped in 2022, thus avoiding two thousand tons of single-use plastic. Impressive stats to be sure. But also, total bullshit.

I noticed how the video on D&AD's website had purposefully avoided calling H&M what it is: a fast-fashion behemoth. To win an award about sustainability, you can't mention that Zara, H&M, and Forever 21, and now new brands like Shein, Boohoo, and Fashion Nova, only work if we buy more clothes than we need, simply because the prices are too low to ignore and the styles change every time we turn around.

The strenuously art-directed Instagram ads we see are meant to make us ignore that the fashion industry is one of the world's greatest environmental blights, accounting for about 10 percent of carbon emissions and 20 percent of global wastewater.

1 "Building the Foundation to Catalyze Change," D&AD video, 2021, https://www.dandad.org/awards/professional/2021/234928/building-the-foundation-to-catalyze-change/.

The climate crisis might never have gotten so bad without fast fashion. Today, people in the United States buy a new piece of clothing every five days, and we throw away two out of every three things we buy. The volume of what we throw away has doubled in the last twenty years, which you might remember is about when Zara and Forever 21 started appearing at your local mall. In 2021, outside of Accra, the capital of Ghana, a mountain of thrown-away clothes was emitting so much methane that it exploded, then smoldered for months.

No amount of paper packaging is going to change that. The lie goes too deep. Designers have been telling themselves the lie for so long that they don't notice it anymore: the lie that "new" means "better" and "newest" means "best." Climate change has come for us, driven by a culture that views consumption as the key to happiness and a better life. Yet now, what was once seen as a necessary innovation—improving people's lives through better design, and in so doing, improving the broader economy—has curdled into a consumer instinct that pushes us to buy more and more, for reasons we can't always articulate. The line between things that we buy because we need them and things we buy because we're taught to need them has nearly disappeared.

We've known this since the 1960s, when Ken Garland wrote the "First Things First" manifesto,* calling for designers to rethink their role in stoking consumerism. We heard it again more recently in Ruben Pater's book *CAPS LOCK* (2021), which dissects the link between capitalism and graphic design. We ignore their insights at our peril, and I suspect it's because we can't imagine how life could be any other way. But things can be different; in fact, they were.

See page 56 to read about the "First Things First" manifesto.

174

Today's mores around consumption began in the Great Depression, and designers played a critical role in creating them. The Great Depression dragged on for so long partly because our understanding of macroeconomics wasn't great. But by the late 1930s, we did grasp a fundamental truth: the economy has always been a confidence game. It's always been about how people feel—what John Maynard Keynes would in 1936 call the "animal spirits" guiding our decisions. If people feel good, they buy things, and that behavior, tallied up across millions of people, creates greater demand. Greater demand means more jobs and higher pay. Which means being able to heat your home and feed your kids.

But in the 1930s, in an era of bank runs and mass homelessness, how could you make people feel good enough that they'd actually want to go out and buy new things they didn't feel like they could afford? You can imagine the sheer relief people would have felt upon hearing someone who seemed to have an answer. And the answer, proposed by various economists and business leaders, was simple. They called it "consumption engineering," which meant creating products in such a way that people felt like they had to have them.

A new breed of design professional sprang up in the 1940s to serve that need. Many of them, like Raymond Loewy and Walter Dorwin Teague, were former advertising creatives who now had the chance to actually invent the stuff they'd been trying to sell on behalf of clients they resented. During an era in which few consumer products had been "designed" by any kind of professional, the new generation of industrial designers remade almost anything they could: washing machines that were easier to clean than ever before; mason jars that were curved so that you could scrape every last bit of food from them; flyswatters with a target on them that made it fun to kill flies.

The modern design profession started with consumption engineering, which was the idea that you could stoke demand through ingenuity. To do so, in fact, was seen as a moral calling for designers in the 1940s, because the Great Depression had taught that generation about the immense suffering that happened when demand sank to a low tide. But consumption engineering was also the origin of a sin that still sits at the heart of our lives today.

People knew about this dynamic in the 1930s, but they thought planned obsolescence was a good thing. Light bulbs and household appliances were designed not to last past a certain point, so that people had to go out and buy more of them, keeping more people employed. If that sounds outrageous, you're not looking hard enough. Planned obsolescence still rules our lives. It animates every Instagram ad you get for some ingenious but inconsequential tchotchke; the shoddy quality of every Shein or Zara outfit that falls apart after a couple of wearings; and the IKEA furniture you buy that ends up at the curb within a year, wearing a sad handwritten note saying, "FREE."

Even if your new iPhone isn't expressly designed to break every year, the marketing of that iPhone is meant to convince you that your serviceable older model may as well be broken. Who doesn't want those five extra megapixels in the camera, or that supercharged chip that makes it so innovative, nothing that great has ever existed before? A constant barrage of marketing has made us addicted to what's next, chasing the fleeting high of a new purchase that wears off all too quickly.

> **"**
> **Design only matters if it can influence our ideals about what's desirable.**
> **"**

176

If any of this sounds like you, please know that none of this is an accusation. This is how I live, too, and I hate it. I buy a new phone more often than I need to, just because. I buy stuff that ends up on the sidewalk far sooner than I promised myself it would. I buy clothes that I end up not wearing. I'm the child of boomers who believe that consumption makes the world go round. Maybe they ruined the world. So did we all. Every new thing you and I buy requires untraceably vast amounts of carbon emissions to produce, and speeds us toward thousand-year droughts and heat waves that happen all the time, unquenchable wildfires, and rising seas.

The answer to all this isn't to become a bearded hermit who grows their own food in soil fertilized by their own doo-doo. The point is: we don't yet know what the answer will be, but we also don't have time to wait.

In June 2022, the UN's climate science agency published a call to consider cutting consumer demand, which is a core premise of degrowth, a new movement based on the seemingly obvious idea that a planet with finite resources cannot sustain ever-increasing consumption. This was shocking, because even just a couple of years ago, degrowth was seen as a fringe idea limited to protest signs at liberal-arts schools. That has changed due to the efforts of organizations such as the Sunrise Movement and activists such as Greta Thunberg, who have had remarkable success in creating the political will to combat climate change. Reuters notes, "As climate change accelerates and supply chain disruptions offer rich-world consumers an unaccustomed taste of scarcity, the theory is becoming less taboo and some have started to ponder what a degrowth world might look like."[2] As to what it

2 Federica Urso and Mark John, "Analysis: Climate Change, Scarcity Chip Away at Degrowth Taboo," Reuters, August 8, 2022, https://www.reuters.com/business/sustainable-business/climate-change-scarcity-chip-away-degrowth-taboo-2022-08-08/.

3 Victoria Masterson, "Degrowth: What's Behind the Economic Theory and Why Does It Matter Right Now?," World Economic Forum, June 15, 2022, https://www.weforum.org/agenda/2022/06/what-is-degrowth-economics-climate-change/.

might look like, the World Economic Forum muses that degrowth "might mean people in rich countries changing their diets, living in smaller houses and driving and traveling less."[3] In other words, degrowth means changing both our behaviors and our expectations. Services such as mobility sharing, and lifestyle choices such as traveling less or living without a car, will have to become mainstream around the world.

We're not going to create change on that scale by telling people what they should be doing and hoping for the best. People don't like eating their broccoli. People especially don't like being told what they *can't* do. For large-scale behavior change to happen, people have to want those changes. That is where design must play a role.

Designers tend to think about design as a process of creating artifacts: posters, apps, chairs, logos, furniture, gadgets. That's true enough, but it's more than that. Design is the transmission of culture and values. It's a vessel by which we speak to other people without words, and the way in which we try to get them to appreciate some better version of the world through something we make. The emergence of our profession in the 1930s can be our guide. Just as designers of that era thought of themselves as inventing a new culture of consumer demand, the designers of the coming era need to think of themselves as inventing a new way of living that doesn't privilege consumption as the only expression of cultural value. At the very least, we need to start framing consumption differently.

Design only matters if it can influence our ideals about what's desirable—the futures we want. As designers, we need to be engaging our imaginations on a greater scale. Instead of imagining how to make a better widget, we should be dreaming about remaking our willfully ignorant acceptance of consumer culture. But to do that, we must reckon with the assumptions built into the work we do. Today, how many of us work at building up recognition for brands that make disposable crap? How many of us work at building equity for companies who've never had to pay for the damage they've done to society? I'm thinking of the millions minted by the branding company behind BP's bullshit greenwashing, or the millions more minted by the product designers who rethought H&M's plastic packaging and then proudly touted H&M's commitment to being green.

Designers have to show us a better way. What might a fashion brand built on the values of repair and reuse look like? Or a consumer electronics brand built on the notion of making your phone last as long as possible? There are economists who think that degrowth is a ridiculous idea, and that the only way to ensure social cohesion is through doubling down on late-stage capitalism. But why do we accept that this is the only possible world we can make? Why do we accept that greater consumption is the only path toward greater happiness? Consumer culture had to be invented; designers helped invent it. If that's the case, then we can invent something better. We don't have a choice. As designers, we don't have to wait.

Can We Design a More Perfect Union?

by Perrin Drumm

ORIGINALLY PUBLISHED WINTER 2018

Back in the late 1700s, the Industrial Revolution
swept over Europe and the United States, moderniz-
ing practically all means of production in its path.
The way we made things—and the role of the people
making them—would never be the same again.
Workers faced increasingly inhumane conditions:
grueling shifts, poorly maintained (and fire-prone)
buildings, children on the factory floor. The violations
by today's standards are too long to list. But the only
reason those standards exist is because a group of
people with the same axes to grind decided to join
forces and lobby for change.

As the nature and conditions of work evolve,
so must the regulations that protect the worker,
and it hardly ever happens without a fight. Or a strike.
From railroad workers, to cigar rollers, to teachers,
to Hollywood screenplay writers, the history of labor
protest spans practically every industry imaginable.
But the one thing those workers all have in common
is that they were part of a labor union.

Now, with the rise of the freelance worker, the
nature of work has shifted yet again. Never before
have there been so many highly skilled, wholly
unprotected workers in the increasingly unregulated
creative industries. These are the people who design
the products and technology you surround yourself
with every day, from the brand of coffee you brew
each morning to the apps that keep you scrolling
into the night.

Unlike other industries, the hours for these
workers are punishingly long, with all-nighters considered the norm, not the exception. There are no
salary minimums, so people at the same level earn
radically different wages. For freelancers, the list of
grievances grows longer, with issues around health
care and parental leave. But designers are nothing

if not problem solvers, and for such a solutions-oriented group, it struck us as incongruous that they couldn't figure this whole labor-rights-organizing thing out. Perhaps all the designers needed was a ringleader, someone to get them together in a room so they could 1) see that they weren't alone, 2) form a unified collective, and 3) start making the change they so wanted to see. Easy-peasy, right?

Back in 2018, we, the editors at *Eye on Design*—trained in journalism yet completely new to the world of labor organizing—tried to start a graphic design union. The younger designers we gathered were optimistic, but we had some words of warning from the older generation, which boiled down to: graphic designers are by nature solitary workers. Good luck getting a self-interested, siloed work-force to agree on anything. But we were younger and more optimistic then. What if we could help break down those silos? It was worth a try.

While our intentions were good, our results were...less than. Anyone who bore witness to the Google strike or the media-worker struggles in the intervening years knows that even rallying a group of like-minded folks within the same parent company/adversary (Condé Nast, *Gizmodo*, *BuzzFeed*, etc.) is a yearslong, emotionally exhausting slog. But it can be done. Organizing a large and disparate group of freelance workers, however, requires major resources. If we had an extra forty hours a week to play with, we'd look to the film industry's union system, which is com-posed of thousands of creative workers organized into specific fields (directing, cinematography, art department, grips, gaffers, and so on) under the umbrella of IATSE (International Alliance of

182

Theatrical and Stage Employees). It's rife with inequities and inefficiencies, but that's precisely what makes it such a perfect model to learn from. Every IATSE failure to advocate for its members is a lesson for the next wave of union leaders in other creative fields—as with our earnest yet impotent attempt to rally designers. Let us give you a leg up in that fight with a primer on what you might encounter.

4 Joe Allen, "20 Years On, What the UPS Strike Can Teach Us about Reviving a Dying Labor Movement," *In These Times*, August 4, 2017, https://inthese times.com/article/ ups-strike-teamsters- labor-movement-workers.

5 Bob Herbert, "A Workers' Rebellion," *New York Times*, August 7, 1997, https://www.nytimes. com/1997/08/07/ opinion/a-workers- rebellion.html.

"You look around and it's hard to find real full-time work anymore. How do people expect you to make it?" said Linda Borucki, a part-time worker for the past thirteen years.[4] Fellow part-timer Laura Piscotti put it more bluntly: "These companies all have a formula. They don't take you on full-time. They don't pay benefits. Then their profits go through the roof."[5]

While both statements could easily have been made by designers working today, Borucki and Piscotti were members of the Teamsters union during the 1997 UPS strike, which went down as one of the most significant strikes in US history. It took place during the supposed economic boom of the Clinton administration. Yet despite the president's vow to help the working class, "he broke every major promise to the labor movement and regularly used his authority to prevent workers from striking,"

6 Joe Allen, "When Big Brown Shut Down: The UPS Strike Ten Years On," *International Socialist Review*, no. 55 (November–December 2007), https://isreview. org/issues/55/bigbrown/.

7 Allen, "When Big Brown Shut Down."

8 A. Sloan, "Corporate Killers: Wall Street Loves Layoffs. But the Public Is Scared as Hell," *Newsweek*, February 26, 1996, 44–48.

9 Gallup, "The Gig Economy and Alternative Work Arrangements," 2018, https://acrip.co/ contenidos-acrip/ gallup/2020/mayo/ gallup-perspective-gig- economy-perspective- paper.pdf.

wrote author Joe Allen in a piece looking back at the UPS strike.[6] From 1993 to 1995, more than eight and a half million people lost their jobs as a result of corporate downsizing and mergers. Clinton's first secretary of labor, Robert Reich, later admitted that the White House "collaborated [with] and responded to the business community."[7] Sure, there was a boom for Wall Street, but as *Newsweek* noted in 1996, "The public is scared as hell."[8] But they weren't powerless. There was one large organization on the workers' side that knew how to talk down corporate bullies and lobby in DC for legislative change.

Recently David Weil, former administrator for the US Department of Labor's Wage and Hour Division under President Obama, noted some eerily similar economic trends between then and now. Today, a growing number of companies are cutting costs by using contract workers, whose rights to fair wages and overtime compensation are more likely to be violated than those of their full-time counterparts. Data from the Freelancers Union (which, confusingly, isn't technically a union) indicates that this shift toward "alternative work arrangements" means that as many as fifty-five million people, or one-third of the US workforce, is made up of freelancers and independent contractors. And we can expect it to increase to 50 percent in just two years.[9]

If that number seems high, consider that in 1996, two-thirds of UPS's quickly expanding workforce was part time, with a staggering 83 percent of new jobs going to part-timers. Meanwhile, UPS was reporting profits of more than $1 billion, a company record it was expecting to beat in 1997. And yet its part-timers hadn't seen a pay raise since the 1980s; wages were still hovering around eight dollars an hour. There were other grievances, too, such as the lack of job security and a pension plan that UPS was threatening to dip into. By the summer of 1997, with union negotiations going nowhere, 185,000 Teamsters across the country decided to go on strike.

For nearly three weeks, they hoisted picket signs painted with slogans like "UPS means Under-Paid Slaves" and "Part-time America won't work." Packages piled up in warehouses around the country, and other carriers couldn't keep up with the overflow. Support from the media, the public, and other unions poured in. "The rally felt like being at a revival— a revival for the entire, long-beleaguered US labor movement....It was the biggest multi-racial strike in a generation that traversed what we now call the 'Blue State-Red State' divide."[10] After UPS lost approximately $800 million, it grudgingly agreed to create ten thousand full-time jobs, authorize the largest wage increase in the company's history, offer protection against subcontracting union jobs, and promise to leave the full-time pension fund intact. It was a huge, hard-won victory, but it didn't exactly make life easier for the union. As he walked out of their final talks, the UPS chief negotiator whispered to the union leader, "You're dead...and you will pay for this, you son of a bitch."[11]

To be fair, many union negotiations are civil and handled by the book, but it's the heated and dramatic conflicts that make history—and history has an uncanny way of repeating itself. Take our friends in the parcel and shipping industry. You think they've learned anything from the UPS strike? Amazon is currently being sued by contract drivers who want employee status, and FedEx just went through a round of similar lawsuits that cost it almost $250 million. Now that the gig economy is bringing issues like fair wages, benefits, and job security to a head

10 Joe Allen, "The UPS Strike, Two Decades Later," *Jacobin*, August 4, 2017, https://jacobin.com/2017/08/ups-strike-teamsters-logistics-labor-unions-work.

11 Allen, "The UPS Strike, Two Decades Later."

across many industries, workers in every sector, from Teamsters to the tech industry, are making a case for better employment packages, and employers are finally starting to respond. Design, and any industry where designers work—media, advertising, publishing—is next in line.

It's not about quelling the demands of independent contractors while giving preferential treatment and heaps of benefits to full-timers and full-timers only. It's not about fighting against the freelance business model, either. It's not even always about fighting the unions—it's about new competition, too. There are just too many other companies offering a quality work experience for full-timers, part-timers, and gig workers alike for anyone to accept a raw deal anymore. That means the bargaining power is shifting to the workers, but their efforts are scattered at best.

Rather than try to patch up the inevitable splintering of the workforce or force an outdated union model to work, might it not be a better use of our time, and in our best interest, to find a way to offer benefits and simply protect people who work, no matter where, when, how often, or what they're called? As problem solvers personally invested in this problem, might not designers be best suited to solve it?

This isn't as idealistic as it seems. Weil, of the Obama administration, is a fan of portable benefits that would essentially follow a worker wherever they go. He's also optimistic that such a proposal could win bipartisan congressional support and even improve the president's approval rating. "If the president-elect is serious about fighting for these workers, I would hope he and his appointees would take on these causes in a creative way that ultimately gets back to the principles of protecting workers in a way our laws have always stated," he said in an interview with *Fast Company*.[12]

As quickly as the labor force has changed in recent years, it's only going to keep changing. As soon as 2030, we can apparently expect AI to compose a whopping 50 percent of the workforce. Whether that happens or not, one thing that's clear is that the way we classify workers will become outdated almost as soon as we can all agree on terms. If we apply obsolete rules to this new workforce, then the fifty-five million freelancers of today will become the hundreds of millions of beleaguered, lawsuit-threatening strikers of tomorrow. It's vital for both workers and companies to be protected. While forming a union might not be the best option for the design industry, there's certainly a lot designers can learn from what the union model gets right and what it gets wrong.

The first surprising lesson? Unions aren't as outmoded as you might think. When digital writers at *Vice*, MTV, *HuffPost*, *Gizmodo*, and *The Intercept* recently sought higher wages, editorial protections, and benefits for part-time workers, they joined the Digital Writers Union in partnership with the Writers Guild of America, East (WGA-E) and used the power of collective bargaining to enact real change. "People were fed up and broke and anxious about the future, and the union gave them a way to take control and force things to change," said Kim Kelly, an editor for *Vice*'s music and culture site, *Noisey*, in an interview with the *New York Times*.[13]

The WGA-E's executive director, Lowell Peterson, recognizes that while unions carry negative baggage for an older generation familiar with the highly publicized stories of corrupt leaders from the

12 Ben Schiller, "Obama's Chief Labor Standards Enforcer Wants the Gig Economy to Work for Workers," *Fast Company*, January 11, 2017, https://www.fastcompany.com/3066798/obamas-chief-labor-standards-enforcer-wants-the-gig-economy-to-work-for-workers.

13 Matthew Sedacca, "Unions Are Gaining a Foothold at Digital Media Companies," *New York Times*, December 26, 2017, https://www.nytimes.com/2017/12/26/business/media/unions-digital-media.html.

14 Lowell Peterson, "Collective Bargaining in the Digital Workplace," *HuffPost*, June 5, 2015, https://www.huffpost.com/entry/collective-bargaining-in_b_7519428.

15 James Warren, "Vox Media Workers' Union Move, Explained," *Poynter*, November 27, 2017, https://www.poynter.org/business-work/2017/vox-media-workers-union-move-explained/.

16 Hamilton Nolan, "A Billionaire Destroyed His Newsrooms Out of Spite," *New York Times*, November 3, 2017, https://www.nytimes.com/2017/11/03/opinion/dnainfo-gothamist-ricketts-union.html.

1960s and 1970s, that doesn't faze a younger workforce. "Perhaps it is true that archaic stereotypes of unions—you know, rigid institutions bent on imposing clunky rules to hamstring the world's job creators—would not seem to have any appeal for workers who deploy wit, are tech-savvy, and rely on creativity and nimbleness rather than brawn and routine," he said in a *HuffPost* article. "But the commonplace notion of retrograde unions ignores the reality of the modern labor movement, which has thought long and hard about how to adapt to the contingent, flexible economy of the twenty-first century, and to the real needs of the modern workforce."[14]

It runs counter to "assumptions about younger Americans' lack of interest in such collective action and the inability of unions to lure white-collar millennials," as *Poynter*'s James Warren puts it.[15] Media companies that are betting against this "mini-trend" may soon find themselves on the wrong side of history. At the time of this publication, Vox Media refused to follow in the footsteps of other editorial sites and acknowledge its writers' union, so the digital media staff staged a series of strikes—not by taking to the streets and refusing to work for days on end, but by boycotting Slack and Twitter for specific hours. They are hoping to reach a resolution soon.

For every new union gain, however, there's a setback. When the writers at DNA*info* and *Gothamist* voted twenty-five to two in favor of unionization, the sites' owner, Joe Ricketts, closed the entire operation, sparking headlines like this in the *New York Times*: "A Billionaire Destroyed His Newsrooms Out of Spite."[16]

Unions tend to gain power in times of economic uncertainty, and decline during economic upswings or once an industry's specific need has been met. As a country, the United States saw unions decline during the Roaring Twenties and then rise again during the Great Depression. In a precarious economy, where sudden sweeping changes from the government or a mercurial start-up founder could mean the loss of a job, hours, benefits, or a pension, today's young, agile, community-oriented workforce is finding strength in numbers. If digital media writers can do it, can designers, too?

Allan Chochinov, chair of School of Visual Arts' MFA in Products of Design, thinks designers are up to the challenge. "If clients treated designers well this wouldn't even be a thing. Unions are a monopolization, but have we reached the point where employers have asked for this?" he says. "There are great studios, of course, but we're approaching levels of workforce abuse where designers are signing away IP to big companies, there are overreaching contracts, 20 percent time, permalancing gone mad—and with no hope of benefits. We hear a lot about how the gig economy is good for designers who want flexibility, but it's really only good for management, who never has to look after anyone again."

Darryl Mascarenhas, a partner at the creative agency Lively Group, acknowledges that workforce abuse is rife at agencies, where designers are often working against tight deadlines. "Some agencies don't care because they're under client pressure and will just move on to the next designer. But take a group like [freelance talent agency] Working Not Working, which a lot of agencies use. Those people don't get run into the ground because it'll get around. I suppose unions could upgrade declining payment rates and provide things like insurance and 401Ks, but the structure of a union would have to change; it's just so outdated. Maybe the general designer should just learn their worth and how to negotiate their rates."

In an industry where it's easy to be taken advantage of, most designers and illustrators become accustomed to looking out for themselves. "When I was starting off, I worked around the clock for teeny amounts and with no idea what work was valued at," says illustrator Wendy MacNaughton. "When I started working with a commercial agent, which I don't anymore, I learned more about how rights work, about limitations and renewals, things like that. Having understood that earlier would have been helpful. We all struggle with valuing ourselves and figuring out how to charge, especially early on. If there was some kind of floor, that would be helpful, especially for women illustrators, who tend to undervalue our work."

MacNaughton also notes that for artists and designers who value autonomy and independence in their work life, being a part of a union can mean more compromise than they're used to. "Am I worried about losing some independence for the good of the group? Of course. But I also realize it's worth it. Our field has changed so much in the past ten to twenty years; maybe it's due for a restructuring that benefits all its members, not just the favored few."

Maria Rapetskaya, creative director of design studio Undefined Creative, is more skeptical still. "Pay regulations would be great, in theory. Most small companies I know are such fragile ecosystems that heavy-handed, broad-strokes regulation would decimate our operations. Our rates and pay structures are intimately tied to our specific sector, our client base, our average budgets, and our production cycles. For example, instead of merit increases, we instituted cost-of-living raises and profit sharing to ensure that everyone gets a really nice end-of-year bonus to boost overall earnings without endangering the financial solvency of the company year-round with salaries. On top of that, rates don't always translate to the quality of work or creativity, speed, efficiency, communication, et cetera. So I'll gladly pay more for freelancers who may be less qualified on paper, but are a fantastic fit. Unfortunately, we've also paid high rates requested by artists who appear exceptionally qualified and then can't deliver. Creativity is far too subjective to be standardized.

"The real problem of the creative industry as I see it isn't that we can't pay fair salaries; the problem is in the perceived value of our services that's been spiraling down. That's a 'buyer side' issue, and isn't something you can regulate with unions. Buyers who want cheap services would go directly to non-union artists, driving pricing down further among small businesses that can't navigate yet another set of bureaucratic hurdles and expenses."

That's only true if we carry the baggage of existing unions with us. If traditional unions might provide value to designers but traditional union models are out of date—and we're talking about designers here—why can't we assess the major problems and design an optimal organizing body for our industry? What if we treat the problem of fair wages and better working conditions like a design brief?

Here, we'll start you off. These are just a few of the current problems to consider:

- Designers have a hard time negotiating their rates. Pay rates and scales are not made readily available.
- Designers have a hard time negotiating terms and scope with clients. There is no visible general consensus on project standards and timelines.

- Design interns are often unpaid, or choose to work for free in exchange for a learning experience that is not delivered.
- Designers often work crazy hours. It's assumed that a designer will work around the clock before a deadline without receiving equivalent time off, for example.
- The value of design is not perceived by those outside the industry like it is for other creative professions (e.g., architects, film directors, actors, writers, etc.).

"

Having a revolution is not in the graphic design DNA.

"

If this doesn't describe your experience or your company, that's great. Unfortunately, it's a reality for many, especially at the junior level. And if you have had a more positive experience, all the more reason to show your support for fair standards that regulate bad actors in the industry. By joining together with hundreds and thousands of other designers and creative professionals, "you gain the muscle of collective action," says Hoyt Wheeler, a professor emeritus at the University of South Carolina who's now a labor arbitrator. With that muscle you can negotiate wages, health and safety issues, benefits, and working conditions with management.

That same muscle can constrain members, too. The flip side of job security is that union members sacrifice individuality by belonging to a group. You may disagree with some of the union's decisions, but you are bound by them. When design expert Steve Heller was the art director of the *New York Times*, he was obliged to be part of a union he couldn't wait to get out of. "You're essentially stuck with a bunch of other people that you're not agreeing with all the time," he says. "What will strength in numbers actually accomplish? Having a revolution is not in the graphic design DNA."

Whether or not you agree with that statement, or are at least more optimistic, the history of union friction has shown that getting broad acceptance among a large group of people, or simply "joining together," isn't simple at all. Plus, design "lacks the history of film unions, for instance," says Heller. "We'd be starting from scratch, which is problematic and requires the education of lots of people, from small to big businesses. There's a logistical problem there."

Few people know firsthand just how complicated these logistical problems are better than Ric Grefé, who was the executive director of AIGA for twenty years and oversaw its growth from a small New York–centric club to a nationwide organization. "If you become a union, you become an enemy," he says. "Historically, union members can become intractable when it comes to employers. Unions work well for freelancers who feel they have no rights, but what's good for the freelancers is bad for the studios, and if AIGA became a union it would be caught in the middle while attempting to represent both."

Without this kind of bargaining power, AIGA offered the salary survey as a means of disclosing pay rates to better inform those working across the industry. At best, nonprofits like the AIGA, or like the Freelancers Union, can create resources for their members and advocate on their behalf, but they can't set regulations or enforce preexisting ones. "The best thing AIGA can do," says Grefé, "is establish a perception of designers that is up the value chain in terms of concept, strategy, and being multidisciplinary, so they can have a greater influence with their clients. It's better to have a moral high ground than lock clients into a union agreement."

Moral high grounds are fine and good, but unless it's in the contract, it's often as good as forgotten. Also, might not a regulated set of professional standards actually improve the public perception of the value of design, as it has for other unionized creative industries, like film and TV? "At one point unions were looked upon as godsends," says Heller. "They set standards. Belonging to a union was a validation of someone's abilities. Personally I'd like to see an organization that has certain standards, and in order to be part of that organization you have to fulfill those standards, through an apprentice period, like architects."

SVA professor Chochinov also sees the value in requiring graphic designers and illustrators to meet a basic requirement for practice. "Short of licensing a profession, could there be a set requirement?" he wonders. "Then benefits like collective bargaining start to become interesting, because there's a guarantee of competency and quality." So, not a union, and not professional license, but an industry-wide standard of proficiency? Sounds kind of like a guild.

Guilds date back to 1080 but rose to prominence in the fourteenth century, when a young person was required to apprentice under a master for a set length of time before they were admitted to the guild and thus marked as a professional. "I like the idea of a guild more than a union," says Mascarenhas. "For the amount of people who claim to be designers, the percentile you'd want to work with is actually pretty low. It's one thing to kern some type, but it's another thing to understand a brief and know how to collaborate with a team. My main questions about a guild would be: Does it fit into the modern working world, and when that changes, can it adapt over time?"

194

Still, a guild can only make recommendations that its membership can use to develop a standard— it can't legally enforce them. So how do we hold people accountable?

We could start by asking designers to hold themselves accountable by opting into an oath of sorts, or some kind of design manifesto. All independent contractors and business owners who vowed to adhere to these standards could mark themselves as "Design Oath Compliant" on their sites, and anyone who didn't proclaim themselves as "proudly DOC" would incur wrath on Twitter. Enforcement by public shaming might even be more powerful than enforcement by unions. Plus, who doesn't love a good acronym?

Of course an oath isn't enough, not by a long shot. If we can learn anything from the shortcomings of medieval guilds or the mistakes made by twentieth-century unions, it's that a new model is needed— something that takes the working parts of all these collectives and leaves the broken bits behind.

"You know, if you really wanted to do design a service after you're done writing about this," says Chochinov, "you could prototype a working model." Anyone good at group logistics?

The Power of Salary Transparency

MADELEINE MORLEY

https://aigaeod.co/
salarytransparency

Since December 2019, more than twenty-eight hundred designers have anonymously disclosed their earnings to the public in an open-source document* that *Eye on Design* released online. Inspired by similar initiatives across media, art, and advertising, we created the spreadsheet to encourage open conversations about money. Eliminating salary speculation helps narrow gender and race pay gaps, and it pressures managers to create clearer rationales for compensation.

When it comes to negotiating, employers tend to hold all the cards. It's often in their interest to keep rates opaque, given that they can't always justify salary differences. Job listings are regularly elusive about compensation even though creatives are more likely to apply to a job if the salary is disclosed.

The information designers added to our salary transparency sheet provides specific insights into the wages of graphic design workers at a range of companies and institutions. According to its findings, for instance, a Pentagram entry-level graphic designer in New York City earns $45,000 annually, a Refinery29 design intern earns $31,000, a New York–based senior designer at Penguin Random House earns $65,000, and a senior visual designer at Google earns $182,000.

Perhaps unsurprisingly, the number of women who submitted salaries to the form is nearly double that of men. The survey's findings also highlight a number of drastic pay gaps between leadership roles and other skilled workers. For example, a graphic designer at Nike reports earning $90,000, while a design director earns $200,000. As Design Action Collective and Partner & Partners have written for us in the past, there's a prevalent and "inverted relationship between the executive class, who hold the decision-making power, and the young, hungry underlings who execute much of the labor."[17]

Disclosing your salary to a colleague can be more than just uncomfortable—it may be viewed as a subversive act. Most companies work hard to keep pay opaque, and studios, agencies, institutions, and companies are increasingly savvy when it comes to omitting wage information. As our online spreadsheet continues to grow, we hope the wage gap continues to wane.

17 Design Action Collective and Partner & Partners, "Every Design Studio Should Be a Worker-Owned Studio," *Eye on Design*, October 25, 2021, https://eyeondesign.aiga.org/every-design-studio-should-be-a-worker-owned-studio/.

Welcome to the Designer's Club— Keep Out

by Khoi Vinh

ORIGINALLY PUBLISHED DECEMBER 11, 2019

It can be hard to track how design as a profession is evolving day to day, but just a few years after writing this piece on design's tendency toward insular shoptalk, it's apparent that so much has changed. At first, design continued along the same path, turning even more inward. There was an emphasis on more and more intricate tools and processes, while leaving to others the work of engaging with the wider public on the impact of our profession. Recently, though, due to circumstances outside of our control but nevertheless predictable, things have started looking very different.

Artificial intelligence, long advertised but slow to deliver, suddenly caught up to the creative arts with tools like DALL-E 2, Midjourney, Stable Diffusion, and others. Suddenly the articulation of an artistic idea has become virtually the same as its execution. At the moment, this technology seems focused on the expressive visual arts, like illustration, photography, and imaging, but it doesn't take a great mental leap to imagine this sort of innovation being applied to the work designers do every day. More to the point, it could liberate the work product of designers from designers themselves, thereby opening the means of the craft to anyone able to type what basically amounts to a search engine query.

How will the profession cope with this disruption? How will people continue to value what designers think when their output might soon seem even more weightless than it has in the past? These questions are going to become very urgent very soon, and for better or worse, the profession will have to contend with how much, or how little, it has explained itself to the world at large.

esigners like to think design is an amazing, transformative force for the betterment of the human condition. But the rest of the world doesn't see it this way. Not that there's vehement opposition to that idea; rather, much of the population is oblivious to design's relevance. Why is that? This question is a pivotal one for the profession. Understanding the gap between how designers see our work and how society values it will determine how we practice our craft for the next several decades— at least. It's the difference between accepting design as a small, insular culture, and design living up to its promise as something that can change the human experience. To that end, it's useful to examine how the practice of design—specifically, creating interfaces to technology—compares with the practice of engineering—constructing the technology. The two are inextricably linked, but the nature of their divergence is striking.

Those who aspire to write code know that there's a virtually limitless number of ways to study engineering. Even outside of the halls of "traditional" computer science programs, there are countless books and online resources that teach any flavor of coding. Even Apple, perhaps the world's most successful purveyor of design, actively encourages people to learn how to code using its Swift programming language. On the company's website, they promote resources for studying Swift with the headline "Everyone Can Code"— a beautifully democratic declaration that belies the company's desire to engage developers on its proprietary platforms. But that headline is also telling about the way engineering is valued.

If everyone can code, and if Apple, one of the world's largest companies, is endeavoring to teach us all to do just that, the implications are potentially immense: there are many, many more new engineers on the horizon. Lots of them will likely be hobbyists, but inevitably, lots of them will be entering the field as professionals. The quality of these new engineers will be highly variable. Some of them might become world-class programmers, but many of them will not. Plenty of these new entrants will, as a matter of course, write lots of "bad code." Yet, as a trade and a profession, the world of engineering hardly seems troubled by this. There's no sense of alarm that this potential influx of new practitioners will somehow disenfranchise the incumbent professionals—and no outrage at the likelihood of lots more bad code being written.

In fact, the sentiment among both professional engineers and Western society is that we're not producing *enough* engineers. Among employers, the competition to hire engineers is consistently high, and working engineers are among the most well-positioned to be selective in choosing their own career paths.

All of this is a reflection not just of how the world values engineering, but also of how comfortable the world has become with it. We're all steeped in engineering in some form or another. Not only do we use the products and services that result from it, we also "speak" technology, routinely using words like "reboot," "bandwidth," "offline," and "beta" in all kinds of contexts, technology-related and not. The fact that engineering has become heavily democratized has only made it more integral to our existence and a more powerful force for change.

But designers don't think this way about design. For us, the prospect of more people everywhere doing design is something not to embrace, but to forestall.

18 Mike Monteiro, "Design's Lost Generation," *Medium*, February 18, 2018, https:// monteiro.medium.com/ designs-lost-generation- ac7289549017.

Take, for example, platforms such as 99designs or Fiverr—marketplaces where design is inexpensive and highly variable in quality. Most professional designers regard these as embodiments of a systemic under-valuing of design. But looked at another way, these sites represent opportunities for those without formal Western design training to log valuable experience. They're on-ramps for a wider population to take part in the design process.

Or consider the continually simmering debate over certification, the argument that our profession's "all comers" policy actually tilts the playing field against the most capable. In an emphatically argued article called "Design's Lost Generation," Mike Monteiro, cofounder of Mule Design, contends that modern design problems have become so complex that "we ought to need a license to solve them."[18] This assessment correctly appreciates design's poten-tial to impact the world, but it fails to address the notion that certification is sure to make design even less diverse and inclusive. If you think the profession is white and male now, imagine if we instituted the equivalent of a bar exam.

The list of these misguided objections goes on. But the theme that runs through all of them is a kind of territorialism, a feeling that only "real" designers should be allowed to practice design. All others should stay in their lane.

If we follow the example of engineering, what's clear is that design's protectionist attitude is short-sighted and self-defeating. Where engineering has gone wide, has let the world in, has proliferated its ideas and culture to people from all walks of life, design has done the opposite. It has focused on limit-ing participation, on preserving its perception as a highly specialized craft, and has even exaggerated the mystical nature of the creative process. Out of the belief that we were making design better for ourselves, we've held it down so tightly that it makes little sense to everyone else.

Case in point: If you google the term "tech backlash," you'll get no shortage of links about how society is reevaluating its relationship with technology. There are widespread concerns about access to our personal data, how our devices are impacting our mental health, and the way that our own social activity is essentially being weaponized against us. But if you google the words "design backlash," the results are like a ghost town, with tumbleweeds of irrelevance blowing through. There's nothing about design's role in these challenges, nothing even about design's culpability in creating these problems. To the world at large, these are classified as technology problems, but the answers to these problems are at least as much about design, about putting humane interfaces on powerful technology.

That, as much as anything, reflects how little the world understands design. The question before us now is: Will designers be satisfied with continued marginalization as the world grapples with problems that we helped create—and that we know we can help to resolve? Or are we ready to embrace a radical new view of who can practice design, who can take part in it—and what our own responsibility is to help the world at large understand what design actually is? Only then can design fulfill its potential to be the difference-making, transformative force for change that every designer believes it can be.

The Moodboard Effect

by Elizabeth Goodspeed

ou've seen it before: an isolated medicine cabinet, filled with a range of beautifully packaged products, photographed head-on in front of a flat backdrop. The lighting is bold and bright, as if the whole shelving unit is illuminated from behind by a fluorescent lightbox. The shelves themselves are likely made of glass and steel, providing a certain je ne sais quoi that's integral to the elevated look— a seamless blend of the mundane and the ethereal. This photographic setup, dubbed the "shelfie," began with a 1982 Clinique campaign by Irving Penn. Since then, dozens of brands and publications have adopted the style, transforming it from a brilliant composition to a personal-care trope.

There are many more oft-mimicked setups like the shelfie currently bouncing around the zeitgeist. One omnipresent shot includes objects placed on a mirror reflecting a cloud-filled sky, giving the illusion of the product floating in midair. Another example uses a dense pattern of water droplets to refract a single subject into a series of psychedelic miniatures. Yet another places subjects in front of faux scenic backdrops reminiscent of a low-budget Sears photo studio. Each of these distinct setups is utilized broadly and in many different markets, with the same composition and concept seen on the Instagram feeds of a major beverage syndicate and an indie skin-care brand alike.

While each of these photographic trends is precise in its particulars, on closer examination, the photos across trends begin to resemble one another

as well; objects start to float against landscape back-drops instead of clouds, and shelves become spotted with dewdrops. It's as if there's a hidden network of identical references hiding behind every image—each shot finding inspiration in the aesthetic com-ponents of the last, like an elaborate game of telephone. Once you start to notice the recurring elements embedded in every "new" compositional approach, it's like a sixth sense (or maybe more like a brainworm) that you can't shut off.

This kind of visual homogeneity is a common occurrence in the creative industry, where ubiquitous styles operate less like trends and more like memes, remixed and diluted until they become a single visual mass. In today's extremely online and results-driven world, the vast availability of reference imagery and the speed with which we encounter it has, per-haps counterintuitively, led to narrower thinking and shallower visual ideation. It's a product of what I like to call the "moodboard effect."

This continuity of specific compositions is especially endemic in the art-direction world. Unlike in graphic design, where client approval usually happens after work has been created, in art direction, the order is flipped, with client approval required before any imagery has been made. This gap between sign-off and execution is where the mood-board comes in: art directors are expected to provide a variety of boards that break down nearly every aspect of a shoot (from lighting to propping) as well as to provide a shot list of intended captures. This pressure to provide final results in advance of produc-tion encourages art directors to only propose ideas that they can find existing photographic examples of and to ultimately re-create these ideas in some way on set, no matter that for much of the past, simple sketches or written descriptions of shots were more than adequate to demonstrate an intended visual result.

The dispersion and parceling out of creative labor inherent to art-direction projects is another factor limiting new approaches in commercial photography. Once a designer has gotten approval from the client, they provide a brief, often in the form of an annotated moodboard, to the other collaborators on the project. Each participant's ability to ideate is limited to solutions that fit within these visual frameworks they've been given, rendering an ostensibly collaborative process far more hierarchical. In my conversations with prop stylists, scenic designers, and photographers about art-direction trends, many have reported that they felt uncomfortable being asked to copy a certain motif from a found image, but didn't feel they had the ability to push back. Each seemed to place the blame on another member's request, and feared being the squeaky wheel (an anxiety bolstered by the precarity of being a freelancer employed through word of mouth). The result: prop stylists acquiesce their creative decisions to photographers, photographers to art directors, art directors to clients, and everyone to the moodboard—with the responsibility for breaking the chain of repetition getting lost in the ether between them.

Unfortunately, while the problem of tight repetition is especially common in art direction, it certainly expands into other creative specializations. In design and branding, mimicry and trope cycling are increasing as well, with certain motifs like fruit-sticker-style graphics or in-line iconography usage running rampant across industries. As in art direction, repetition in design is often the result of client requests and a warped preapproval process driven by moodboards.

The rising number of small creative studios across the globe has created a more competitive marketplace, allowing clients to ask agencies for spec work—usually in the form of an RFP—that shows a potential final result for a project before it has even formally kicked off. Like the pre-shoot photo moodboard, the time constraints and low- or no-budget circumstance of these RFPs encourage designers to build their solutions from a collage of existing design work, giving them little room to play outside the moodboard upon winning a bid.

On top of this, expanded public awareness of graphic design and "design thinking" in pop culture has led to more client involvement in the design process itself. Clients increasingly arrive to project kickoff with their own moodboards, many of which draw from successful brands within their industry. These competitors' successes are conflated with their use of certain design motifs, which clients then ask to replicate within their own brand. Designers are expected to use these client moodboards as the foundation beneath their own work, which often results in an output that feels like a remix rather than a fresh idea.

Repetition within visual culture is a common phenomenon. Anyone who has studied art history has seen the vast number of motifs and ideas that pass through the commercial and fine-art world over time. In fact, the very way that most of us learn the history of visual art and design is through a parade of neatly partitioned art movements—an organizational method that, at best, can help us better analyze and understand visual culture at a given time in history.

But art movements are networked tendencies or styles deployed in service of a distinct ideology. They are typically a response to a specific time, place,

> "
> **Ubiquitous styles operate less like trends and more like memes.**
> "

series of events, or previous way of making. The use of certain palettes, forms, or techniques within these movements, like in Dadaism or Art Nouveau, is irrevocably connected with a line of thought, which is often further codified in the form of a manifesto or the internal rules of an artist collective. What's distinct about contemporary visual trends, on the other hand, seems to be the consistency with which particular combinations of formal tropes recur, combined with a detachment from the meaning behind those forms. Unlike art movements, modern aesthetic trends are lacking in connective philosophical tissue; they operate instead on a surface level, rendering form without function. Their only commonality is commerce—they're designed in an effort to make money for a company.

The way in which images are selected and placed within the context of a moodboard is, in my opinion, the primary driving force behind the divorce of surface appearance and deeper logic, and the resulting visual monotony seen in much contemporary design. In an interview with *The Brand Identity*, Jesse Reed, cofounder of the New York design studio Order, reiterated this idea and communicated his studio's distaste for moodboarding: "Moodboards result in visual derivatives.... Leading with aesthetic influences as opposed to meaningful connections further propels the cycle of sameness."[19]

This problem is further exacerbated by the platforms in which we encounter the mostly contemporary design that serves as our reference material. Art directors and designers, tasked with sourcing imagery to populate their moodboards quickly and precisely, are increasingly turning to collective inspiration websites like Pinterest. On these sites, visual fodder is either served up by algorithms or manually

19 Elliott Moody, "Rules, Relations & Reasons: Presenting a Manifesto for the Graphic Design Industry to Stand By," *Brand Identity*, November 14, 2021, https://the-brandidentity.com/interview/rules-relations-reasons.

bucketed out into thematic folders by users. In the case of the former, where the hand of the curator is replaced by the eye of the machine, collections emerge from binary matching of forms, colors, and compositions; a related image search for a red book on a table tends to turn up more red books, and more books on tables. Like begets like. And while algorithms are often perceived as neutral, they are deeply biased toward the material they've been trained on. This can lead to mainstream aesthetic ideas advancing at a more rapid rate than less common aesthetic ideas (a concept explored in fascinating depth outside aesthetics by Safiya Umoja Noble in the 2018 book *Algorithms of Oppression: How Search Engines Reinforce Racism*). It's no surprise, then, that designers relying on algorithms to provide their references may inevitably find themselves with a moodboard that shows the most popular visual tropes, used in a similar way, toward similar results.

However, even in the case of references found through individual human selection rather than via algorithm, the very UX design of curatorial platforms like Are.na has shifted the way we engage with creative work. A collection-oriented platform forces elements to be identified by a single trait—format, color, medium, or date created—rather than as a unified amalgamation of ideas and aesthetics. By stripping imagery from its in-situ context and pairing it with items that only share a similarity across a single spectrum, it becomes difficult to grasp the conceptual rationale behind their formal appearance. Rather than each piece being seen as the result of a network of overlapping visual and abstract ideas, it's sliced into component elements—it is the sum of its parts instead of a whole. When these borrowed images are further compiled into moodboards, they're so ideologically flattened that it's near impossible to use them as a brainstorming tool for new ideas. They become a rigid road map instead.

While curation is undoubtedly an art form in its own right, to borrow critic Fran Lebowitz's words, a sense of discovery is not equal to invention. The shift toward curation-as-identity, or in start-up lingo, CAAS (curation as a service), has also inflated the perceived value of assembled reference as an end product rather than a tool to create new work. In addition to flattening the ideological and conceptual rationale behind design decisions, this mode of collecting-as-art also has a peculiar way of transferring and removing authorship (see also DALL-E 2 and other AI art), often an integral part of understanding the logic and depth of meaning behind a creation. Designer Mikey Joyce articulated this in a tweet in July 2022, saying that on the internet, "every image is a 'found image'" and "inspiration references are perceived to be open-source assets."

Is the solution to remove references, and moodboards, from our tool kit? Many designers support this view, and claim that avoiding other design work has kept their own output unadulterated. To my mind, this is an impossible feat; daily life in our capitalist, content-saturated world forces us to encounter creative expression whether we like it or not. Even if we avoid engaging with contemporary design via social media or industry blogs, we still confront brand identities at the supermarket, photography in advertisements, and typography absolutely anywhere we look. Anyone who has ever changed their mind about skinny or wide-leg pants knows that folks who say they don't bring outside influence to their work discount the profound impact our environment has on our internal ideas of taste. There's no way we can't consider other work—so we may as well do it thoughtfully and with intention.

The secret is: there isn't anything new, really. Everything is a remix. As such, the paradoxical trick to beating mimicry may be to go in the opposite direction entirely: to look at more references, and make more moodboards. Collecting references and assembling moodboards can be more like stocking a kitchen pantry than filing papers in a file cabinet: it can be a gradual process that brings together items with a common purpose but a diverse range of formats, tastes, smells, and provenance. By engaging with a wider variety of visual material, from a range of industries outside design, regions beyond the West, eras outside the twenty-first century, and via more platforms, including outside digital infrastructures, we give our brains more material to percolate on, and more chances to properly intermingle different and richer ideas, instead of just repeating them.

On Visual Sustainability with Benedetta Crippa

by Meg Miller

https://aigaeod.co/
crippa

enedetta Crippa* is an Italian designer living in Stockholm, where she runs a design studio, teaches, and speaks regularly about her research on "visual sustainability." Long interested in how design can contribute to a more just society, Crippa started thinking seriously about sustainability while working as lead designer at Stockholm Environment Institute, where she made the institute's scientific research on social and environmental sustainability legible for a wider audience through graphics, data visualizations, and consultancy. She has since developed a course called Quantum Thinking: Sustainability in and through Visuality, which she teaches as a guest lecturer at Konstfack University of Arts, Crafts and Design, alongside advising students at Beckmans College of Design. Her richly colorful, densely ornamental work is grounded in feminist and postcolonial design theory and, in her words, works to address that which throughout history "has been stripped of power and authority" and relegated to the margins.

Crippa uses the term "visual sustainability" to demonstrate how graphic design can be sustainable not just through its messaging or materiality, but also through its form. While many designers struggle to reconcile a commitment to sustainability with the demands of their chosen profession, Crippa argues that designers can and should address unethical and exploitative systems through their craft. She compels designers to think about sustainability in terms of designing within boundaries, rather than thinking that the only sustainable solution is to design less

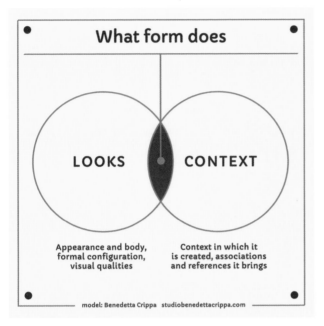

Visualization by Benedetta Crippa.

or not at all. She cautioned when we spoke that visual sustainability isn't just about the environment or climate change—it also challenges and presents alternatives to dominant structures like capitalism, patriarchy, and white supremacy. Below, I talk to Crippa about how she practices sustainability on her terms, and how she encourages her students to define it for themselves.

————

MEG MILLER: There's been a lot of discussion about what it means to have a sustainable design practice in the midst of the climate crisis. What common approaches do you see for achieving this, and how would you like to see people thinking about it?

BENEDETTA CRIPPA: One thing I've observed is that there's been a big focus on reduction. The typical questions are: Do we really need another pair of shoes? Do we really need another website? And so on. This makes sense—we've been consuming too much and haven't been acting in a way that is sustainable for ourselves or for the planet. But when we simply frame sustainability as a question of what we should not do and what we should not design, this leaves design practitioners in a very tough place.

The question I think we should ask instead is: How do we work within certain boundaries? Sometimes these things coincide—to act within the boundaries of the planet right now, we indeed have to reduce. But I think when we shift the narrative from "not designing" to "designing within boundaries," we are empowered rather than suppressed. We are in a position of doing exactly what design is about, which is working within certain constraints. We can then start to prioritize a variety of needs within the ecosystems that we inhabit. This includes recognizing beauty, recognizing creativity, and recognizing art as components that are absolutely essential for coexisting sustainably. If we grow a generation of designers who are acquainted with the idea of designing within boundaries, there can be meaningful, radical, and long-lasting change ahead.

MILLER: When did you begin researching visual sustainability, and how did you come to start using this term for what you were doing?

CRIPPA: While working, I started to notice that even sustainability-savvy clients and established designers were more and more frequently coming up with suggestions where the goal of communicativeness

218

was actually dropped in favor of solutions that were at times questionable, and at times outright problematic. For example, the idea that printing without color is more sustainable, and therefore more ethical. I started to see that the well-intentioned aim of sustainability was paving the way to a narrative where austerity is yet again the "best choice," and I wondered how we could be having a more nuanced and meaningful discussion about sustainability.

Around the same time, I was working at the Stockholm Environment Institute, one of the most respected research institutes on sustainability in the world, and an arts institution in Norway invited me to give a talk for the Global Climate Strike. Since I'm a practicing designer, not an academic, these types of contexts are opportunities to elaborate on research questions, and this created the foundation of the research. After that, I continued to bring the research to a few conferences and international events. I wrote a text called "The Colour of Green," and started to design a model for what I believe sustainable design is. That became the basis for a course on visual sustainability at Konstfack. The idea was to start thinking about how graphic designers are in a position to contribute to a more just world through what we do, which is visual communication, and how we do it.

MILLER: What exactly is visual sustainability, in the way that you use the term?

CRIPPA: It means sustainability carried out through the visual qualities of design. For example, let's say that I use recycled paper for my book. That's fantastic, but that's not visual sustainability because the reader will not know that the paper is recycled unless

> " When we shift the narrative from "not designing" to "designing within boundaries," we are empowered rather than suppressed. "

I declare it. But: Can I put forward certain values through the colors that I choose, or the way the cover is designed? Visual sustainability involves things that do not need to be said because they are directly experienced by anyone interacting with the design. And what I mean by "sustainable" in this context is that the design acts in nonexploitative ways. Rather, it's design that's regenerative and puts forward a greater appreciation for coexistence.

MILLER: How do you advise your students to take that idea and apply it in practice?

CRIPPA: Most of my students arrive at my course already caring deeply about sustainability as a general concept. But many of them have also been told that the best options they have are to design less or not design at all, so they also arrive with a certain level of suspicion—the theme simply turns them off. So first and foremost, I try to bring them back to a place of empowerment, a place that tells them they can use what they've been trained to do, and that in fact it's crucial that they do. They don't need to throw away their design education and go and study environmental development in order to make a difference.

I'm also careful not to point them to a specific style. We should never answer a big question like this with a specific style—that means we're setting an agenda. Rather, I try to reframe their approach to design so that it's grounded in the importance of structural change. You will necessarily design in a sustainable way once you have anchored your choices within an analysis of power, and a history of what design does in regard to this power. My role is to give students the tools to look at sustainability in an entirely different way, and from this place of empowerment—and taking into account the need for structural change—they can find their own way in the door, so to speak.

MILLER: Your own work is colorful, striking, ornamental. It draws influence from folk art and craft, and has a real sense of materiality to it. To me, it feels like it comes from a place of abundance, not scarcity, which is maybe why it feels so different from the immediate image of "sustainable design." Can you talk a bit about that tension—how things like beauty, color, and playfulness have become positioned as opposites of sustainability?

CRIPPA: Color and ornamentation have been part of every culture's history, globally, and actually come from very humble origins and the basic human urge to create and make our surroundings more beautiful. On the contrary, through modern design history, this practice has grown to be considered, on one hand, exclusive (for the rich), and on the other, "too much" against the modernist ideal of the minimalist, "clean" design, which has a direct connection with colonial ideas of form and the perception of unstructured, rich expression as less developed. The late architecture critic Lance Hosey covered at length how sustainability has become the antithesis of beauty through a similar process. Part of the reason is that in the current economy, anything that caters to those intangible needs that are unmeasurable and do not directly create a profit—such as the need for creativity, beauty, and meaningful emotional reward—are the first things we believe to be expendable when we have to "reduce." I'm determined to show a different way that is grounded in greater

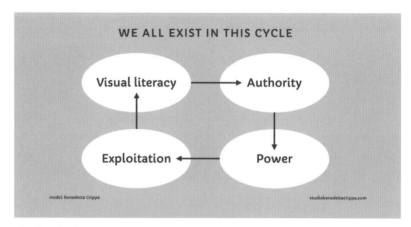

Visualization by Benedetta Crippa.

ownership of our craft and in a holistic critical thinking paired with fine design expertise.

It's also important that we do not land on the conclusion that ethical design looks any specific way. I think no single person should ever take it upon themselves to mark a specific visual expression, color, or composition as expendable, let alone unethical. We should enjoy as diverse a range of visual expressions as we possibly can. Rather than looking a certain way, ethical or sustainable design is guided by an intention to stay within boundaries and to nurture instead of exploit. I do believe that if you design with that intention, this will naturally transpire in the formal configuration of the design.

MILLER: You mentioned that you're not just talking about environmental sustainability. You're questioning how we challenge basic structures—environmental, social, cultural—through form. Why is it important that these things are considered holistically? And why is it important for designers, specifically, to understand these intersections?

CRIPPA: Things haven't always been unsustainable. We are living in a time and place where a long process has led the planet to literally start breaking down. We need to acknowledge the current situation not as something that has always been going on— that could have happened at any time—but as the direct by-product of what I would call a broken promise of coexistence. Humans have broken our silent agreement to coexist with everything around us and the ecosystems we are born into. We have established a system where we exploit not only the planet, but also one another, at a global scale.

If you want to study sustainability, not as a buzzword but as a serious question, this is the baseline to establish first. You need to know how systems intersect. We started with the patriarchy oppressing half of the population. Later, we added colonialism— building a system based on white supremacy over a majority of people of color. To that, we've also added capitalism, which is a system based on endless growth at any cost via consistent exploitation of natural and human resources. Together these three systems have caused the current systemic failure we are experiencing. Going back to the idea of boundaries, patriarchy, white supremacy, and capitalism are all about trespassing boundaries—physical boundaries, emotional boundaries, boundaries of power, boundaries of land, boundaries of reciprocity. We have a small portion of the population that has lived virtually boundaryless at the expense of everybody and everything else.

To reestablish the kind of harmony that sustainability should be about, it is absolutely necessary that we start from understanding these power imbalances. But if I need my students to train in design without taking a degree in social anthropology or environmental science first, I need to find ways to make this clear to them by grounding it in their practice—their practice, not someone else's. Within the course, I have designed some exercises that make as direct a connection as possible between these structures and how things look. This ranges from how Barbie looks to the fact that the color white is the default in most of our modern software—which comes from a Western idea of white being a noncolor, the base to which all else is added. It includes the color pink being considered a "lesser" color because of how it is attached to femininity. And ornamentation being seen as an inferior, unclean type of expression, merely a step toward the superior, minimalistic layout. Once the students make the connection between systems of oppression and how things look, then the point of entry into the practice becomes clear to them. Finally, they're in a place where there's so much they can work with as designers, and can address through their craft, not outside of it.

MILLER: I notice you've recently done some research into how much (or little) investment governments and societies put into visual culture. How does that impact countries in terms of visual literacy, and how could things be different?

CRIPPA: I've become acutely aware of how much the practice of graphic design is underrepresented on an academic research level. It might be because we did not even have graphic design education in most countries until very recently. It might be because graphic designers tend to be practitioners and not academics. But the fact remains that even the most advanced democracies are investing very little in intentional research-based practices in visual communication, graphic design, or visual culture, which would allow us to better understand the crucial importance of visual configurations within social dynamics and systems of power. In Sweden, for instance, the first-ever practice-based PhD position in visual communication was created only in 2021 at Konstfack, and artistic education in Sweden is currently facing heavy budget cuts. During the pandemic the situation got even worse, as investments were diverted even more than usual toward the sciences. We still divide knowledge between "relevant" and "less relevant," and visual culture consistently falls in the latter category. On the contrary, we need to acknowledge it as a fundamental human activity that is worth rigorous study, if we wish for structural change ahead.

With movements like #MeToo and Black Lives Matter in recent years, there's been more of a collective discussion that acknowledges how we create hierarchies among human beings based on how we look. We regularly discriminate between people based on a first layer of information determined by what we see, and this is based, in part, on biological factors, but also vastly on our visual literacy—a socialization we all go through that defines the visual vocabulary we are equipped with, which is specific to the visual culture we are born into, but also features globally shared, constructed ideas—for example the idea that white skin or the male body are superior, better, and more trustworthy. This discussion has highlighted the importance of things like representation, but we're still lacking widespread, accessible research on how visual literacy affects our lives and decision making on a daily basis. I think that the goal of such research would be not to eradicate bias, since that would be impossible, but rather to more precisely understand it, become aware of these processes, educate ourselves on our own blind spots, and create strategies to compensate for that.

When I talk about visual sustainability, I am making this connection between visual literacy and power very clear. It is because of our visual literacy that we keep on confirming certain hierarchies and uphold power imbalances—or create new ones. We need to act on that if we want to create a greater acceptance and celebration of human variety, which also means a variety of ecosystems, a variety of cultures, of expressions, and of ways of existing— in regenerative balance.

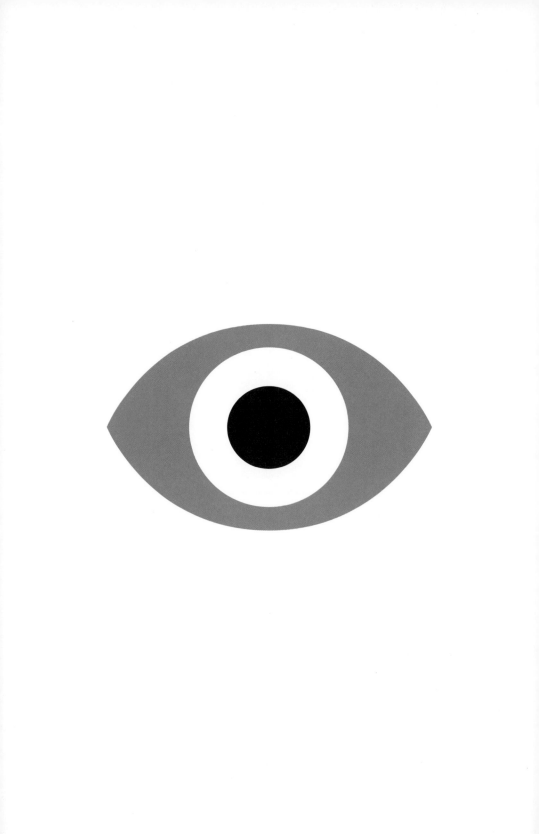

AFTERWORD

When the *Eye on Design* editors sat down to start writing this book, it felt like we were facing a blank page despite having spent the better part of a decade publishing stories about the design world. It was hard to know where to begin. The issue, it seemed, was that there was *too much* to say. From the time when we began to the moment the book was finally finished, so much had already changed.

Design moves at a fast pace—the thinking, the methodologies, and the tools evolve more quickly than many designers can keep up with. Writing a book is so different: it's an effort to suspend time. Or at the very least, it's an effort to capture a moment that feels worth documenting. These two practices might seem at odds, but it's that very tension that we've tried to explore through all of *Eye on Design*'s publishing, including this book.

Looking back, it's clear that we were never actually facing a blank page. In fact, it was the opposite. A website, a magazine, or a book serve as a traceable log—a continual pulse check on what matters to a community at any given point in time. The beauty of keeping an ongoing log is that if you look closely enough, the story is already there. We hope you, our community, found something valuable in the stories we told in these pages.

—*Liz Stinson and Jarrett Fuller, editors*

CONTRIBUTORS

Rachel Berger is a designer, educator, and writer. She served as chair of the Graphic Design Program at California College of Arts from 2014 to 2022.

Perrin Drumm is a writer, editor, and publisher. She founded *Eye on Design* in 2014, and is currently head of publishing at A24.

Jarrett Fuller is a designer, writer, educator, editor, and podcaster. He is an assistant professor of graphic design at North Carolina State University and hosts the podcast *Scratching the Surface*.

Elizabeth Goodspeed is an independent designer and art director who specializes in historically inspired brand, print, and editorial projects. As a writer and educator, she is interested in cyclical patterns in visual culture and the impact of everyday design and ephemera on the larger creative landscape over time.

Sahadeva Hammari is a designer, writer, and entrepreneur living in New York. His work explores the intersection of design, culture, and individual empowerment. He has led design projects at Casetext, Gusto, and Rippling.

John Kazior is an illustrator and author. His writings on the aesthetics of nature in commercial art in the climate crisis have been published in *The Baffler*, *Eye on Design*, MOLD *Magazine*, and elsewhere. Today, he serves as art director at *The Drift* magazine and is a cofounder of the studio Feral Malmö.

Cliff Kuang is a designer working on new paradigms for how we use technology, and the author of *User Friendly: How the Hidden Rules of Design Are Changing the Way We Live, Work, and Play* (2019), which the *New York Times* called an "engrossing tour de force."

Briar Levit is an associate professor of graphic design at Portland State University. Levit's feature-length documentary *Graphic Means: A History of Graphic Design Production* (2016) follows design production from manual to digital methods. She currently codirects the People's Graphic Design Archive with Louise Sandhaus, Brockett Horne, and Morgan Searcy. In 2021, she edited *Baseline Shift: Untold Stories of Women in Graphic Design History*.

Meg Miller is an art and design writer who has contributed to the *New York Times, The Atlantic*, the Creative Independent, Pioneer Works' *Broadcast*, and the *Serving Library*, among others. She is editorial director at Are.na and a contributing editor at Source Type.

Madeleine Morley is a writer and editor based in Berlin and originally from London. Her work focuses on art, design, tech, and culture, and her words have appeared in the *New York Times*, *The Guardian*, *Fast Company*, and *Dazed & Confused*, among other publications. She was previously senior editor at *Eye on Design*.

Rick Poynor is Professor of Design and Visual Culture at the University of Reading in the UK. He is the author of *David King: Designer, Activist, Visual Historian* (2020) and many other publications. His latest book is *Why Graphic Culture Matters: Essays, Polemics and Proposals about Art, Design and Visual Communication* (2023).

Anne Quito is a journalist and design critic. In 2017 she was the first recipient of AIGA's Steven Heller Prize for Cultural Commentary.

Liz Stinson is a writer and editor covering the world of design. She is currently a senior editor at *Fast Company*. She was previously a staff writer at *Wired* and executive editor of *Eye on Design*.

Aggie Toppins is an associate professor and chair of Design at the Sam Fox School of Design & Visual Arts and Washington University in St. Louis. She combines studio practice and critical writing to explore design as a catalyst for social change. Themes in her work include questions of meaning making, activism, and design history's relationship to the practice.

Khoi Vinh has been practicing design in many forms for three decades. He has worked at early- and late-stage tech ventures, media companies, advertising agencies, and more.

ACKNOWLEDGMENTS

Eye on Design is, by its nature, a collaborative effort. It wouldn't exist without the support of AIGA's staff and board, who have long believed in the value of an independently run publication as well as in the necessity of rigorous design journalism and thoughtful design commentary.

Over the years, *Eye on Design* has worked with too many fantastic contributors to name here, but this book wouldn't have been possible without the efforts of *Eye on Design*'s past editorial team, who helped produce all of the stories in these pages. Thank you to Madeleine Morley, whose fingerprints are all over the book; to Meg Miller, who was instrumental in giving the book its structure; to Emily Gosling, who helped hone *Eye on Design*'s voice; to Zac Petit, who shared ideas and feedback on the book; and, of course, to Perrin Drumm, who brought *Eye on Design* to life in the first place.

Major gratitude goes to Tala Safié, whose brilliant design mind gave the book its creative direction and visual form, including bringing on Nejc Prah, who crafted the beautiful illustration work throughout. Safié has been instrumental in establishing *Eye on Design*'s visual language from its earliest days—without her, *Eye on Design* would be far less clever and fun to read.

A big thank you to our editor, Jennifer Thompson; to design director, Paul Wagner, whose idea it was to create an *Eye on Design* book; and to the many writers and illustrators who believed in writing for a small publication, for nonprofit pay, because they wanted to contribute to a place where they could express their thoughts and voices outside of the constraints of traditional media. It's amazing what we've all accomplished together.

CREDITS

31: Courtesy of Molly Baz
39: Black Dog & Leventhal (middle); AUC Press (bottom)
53: Johan Kugelberg hip hop collection, #8021. Division of Rare and Manuscript Collections, Cornell University Library
54: Bauhaus Dessau Foundation I 44148 / loan from Wilma Stöhr (middle); published by American Newsrepeat Co., © Mari Tepper, courtesy of the artist (bottom)
59: © Ken Garland, courtesy of Rick Poyner
60, 61: *Adbusters* no. 23 (1998), courtesy of Rick Poyner
63: *AIGA Journal of Graphic Design* 17, 0. 2 (1999), courtesy of AIGA
71: *Wall Street Journal*, 1989, courtesy of Joe Duffy
72: Courtesy of Joe Duffy (top)
73: Courtesy of AIGA
75: Courtesy of The Monacelli Press
82: Courtesy of John Maeda
83: Courtesy of David Small
86: Courtesy of Golin Levin
89: Courtesy of Casey Reas
104: ©The Renaissance Society at the University of Chicago, photographer Tom Van Eynde
110: © brutalistwebsites.com and original designers, courtesy of Brutalist Websites
111: Mike Joyce, Swissted (various posters), © Mike Joyce, courtesy of the artist

128: Courtesy of Danielle Aubert
129: Courtesy of See Red Women's Workshop
131: Courtesy of Poster Workshop
146: Courtesy of Span
206–7: Collage courtesy of Elizabeth Goodspeed
217: Courtesy of Benedetta Crippa
222: Courtesy of Benedetta Crippa

INDEX

Published by
Princeton Architectural Press
A division of Chronicle Books LLC
70 West 36th Street
New York, NY 10018
papress.com

Editor: Jennifer Thompson
Design concept: Tala Safié
Design and typesetting: Paul Wagner

Typeset in Lyon Text by Kai Bernau
and Maison Neue by Milieu Grotesque

Library of Congress
Cataloging-in-Publication Data
—
Names: Stinson, Liz, editor. | Fuller, Jarrett, editor.
Title: What it means to be a designer
    today : reflections, questions, and ideas from AIGA's Eye
    on design / edited by Liz Stinson and Jarrett Fuller.
Other titles: Eye on design.
Description: First edition. | New York : Princeton Architectural
    Press, [2024] | Includes index. | Summary: "A wide-reaching
    collection of essays and interviews examining the design
    profession and its deep impact on society and culture"
    —Provided by publisher.
Identifiers: LCCN 2023021738 (print) | LCCN 2023021739
    (ebook) | ISBN 9781797224558 (paperback) |
    ISBN 9781797227207 (ebook)
Subjects: LCSH: Design—Social aspects.
Classification: LCC NK1520 .W49 2024 (print) | LCC NK1520
    (ebook) | DDC 744—dc23/eng/20230801 LC record available
    at https://lccn.loc.gov/2023021738 LC ebook record
    available at https://lccn.loc.gov/2023021739